The
DIY Pantry

30 Minutes to Healthy, Homemade Food

Kresha Faber

Avon, Massachusetts

Published by
Adams Media, a division of F+W Media, Inc.
57 Littlefield Street, Avon, MA 02322. U.S.A.
www.adamsmedia.com

ISBN 10: 1-4405-7168-6
ISBN 13: 978-1-4405-7168-8
eISBN 10: 1-4405-7169-4
eISBN 13: 978-1-4405-7169-5

Printed in the United States of America.

10 9 8 7 6 5 4 3 2 1

Library of Congress Cataloging-in-Publication Data

Faber, Kresha.
The DIY pantry / Kresha Faber.
    pages cm
Includes bibliographical references and index.
ISBN-13: 978-1-4405-7168-8 (pb : alk. paper)
ISBN-10: 1-4405-7168-6 (pb : alk. paper)
ISBN-13: 978-1-4405-7169-5 (e-book)
ISBN-10: 978-1-4405-7169-4 (e-book)
1. Cooking (Natural foods) I. Title.
TX741.F33 2013
641.3'02--dc23

2013034870

Always follow safety and commonsense cooking protocol while using kitchen utensils, operating ovens and stoves, and handling uncooked food. If children are assisting in the preparation of any recipe, they should always be supervised by an adult.

Many of the designations used by manufacturers and sellers to distinguish their product are claimed as trademarks. Where those designations appear in this book and F+W Media was aware of a trademark claim, the designations have been printed with initial capital letters.

Cover images © 123rf.com.

This book is available at quantity discounts for bulk purchases.
For information, please call 1-800-289-0963.

Dedication

For my children,
Annika, Evan, and Jonathan

May The Lord bless you and keep you; The Lord make His face shine upon you and be gracious to you; The Lord lift up His countenance upon you and give you peace.

May your bodies ever be nourished with good food and your lives ever be nourished by joy.

Contents

Introduction

With so many grocery stores stocking items that are chock-full of additives, artificial colors, and GMOs (genetically modified organisms), it's becoming nearly impossible to find foods that are healthy and affordable. Thus, The DIY Pantry is meant to be your indispensable, number-one tool in the kitchen to help you fill your home with wholesome, nutrient-rich snacks, mixes, fixings, and meals that will nourish your body. Inspired by traditional methods of cooking, each of the recipes in this book uses simple ingredients, so you can make them in about as much time as it takes to craft a meal from their store-bought counterparts. You'll enjoy all of your favorite foods, from granola bars and biscuits, to baked beans and macaroni and cheese, to caramel sauce and ice cream.

Why Homemade?

Finding whole foods in grocery stores has become more and more difficult with packages often including ingredients that are not only harmful to our bodies but also unidentifiable by the average person. Every single recipe in this book was created with your favorite products in mind as well as your health. To make these as close as possible to the store-brand versions, each recipe was designed and tested with whole food ingredients until it captured as much of those unmistakable flavors as possible. And with 454 recipe testers from around the world, you can be assured that each and every recipe has been tested numerous times over to ensure it's as easy and delicious as it promises to be. Since you see exactly what goes into each recipe, you'll know that each meal is 100 percent real—no high fructose corn syrup, additives, preservatives, GMOs, or fifty-letter chemicals.

Adjust to Your Taste

Since each recipe uses such simple, straightforward ingredients, it's easy to adjust them to suit your preferences. Whether you have a food allergy or don't eat meat, there are plenty of substitutions in this book to help you craft the perfect, all-natural meal or snack. In each recipe, you'll find nutrition facts and easy-to-read icons listing to which diets the recipe adheres. These icons represent the following dietary needs:

 Gluten-Free: Recipe does not include wheat, rye, spelt, Kamut, barley, triticale, graham, semolina, any malt-derived products, or grain alcohol

 Vegetarian: Recipe does not include any meat, including red meat, poultry, or fish. This includes Worcestershire sauce, which is made with anchovies.

 Vegan: Recipe does not include meat or any product made from or by animals

 Dairy-Free: Recipe does not include milk, cream, butter, yogurt, cheese, or any other product derived from cow's milk

 Egg-Free: Recipe does not include whole eggs, egg yolks, or egg whites

Many of the recipes also include information to help you adjust the ingredients to fit your flavor profiles as well, so you'll always know how to make something spicier or milder depending on your tastes. With such a wide range of options for substitutions, you'll always be able to create meals that are immensely satisfying.

Save Money

Commercial pantry staples add up, even if you're an avid coupon user. Stocking up on basic ingredients, however, can ease that budget considerably, especially if you have a checklist of ingredients you purchase regularly and stock up when they go on sale. Each recipe in this book includes a cost rating system that will help you figure out if something is in your budget. This is what each rating represents:

$ = less than 25 cents per serving
$ $ = between 25 cents and 50 cents per serving
$ $ $ = between 50 cents and one dollar per serving
$ $ $ $ = more than one dollar per serving

Remember that while overall it is much cheaper to make your own foods for your pantry, you can't do it all at once without putting a serious dent in your wallet. Be sure to pick and choose recipes as you begin to build your pantry, so that you get the most bang for your buck. Each recipe in this book also breaks down the prep and cook times for the meal as well as its difficulty level. The rating system for the difficulty ranges from "one star" (very easy to make and the ingredients are easy to find) to "four stars" (may involve a tricky technique or includes difficult-to-find ingredients). However, keep in mind that the "four star" recipes are still doable by a novice cook and that the stars merely denote a bit more care and attention—rolling a cracker dough thin without sticking to the table, for example, rather than merely whisking ingredients in a pan.

So what are you waiting for? It's time to get healthy and live free (additive-free!) with *The DIY Pantry*!

CHAPTER 1

Stocking Your Pantry

You'd like to stock your pantry with nutritious foods, but you're not sure where to start. This chapter will help you understand what kinds of foods you'll want to keep on hand so that you'll always have healthy ingredients ready to prepare any meal, as well as what you need to consider when choosing which recipes are best for you, your diet, your schedule, and your budget. Also, note that while it is so incredibly satisfying to make your own pantry staples and to discover new versions of your favorite foods, it can also be overwhelming to stay on top of keeping your pantry stocked. Thus, while there are enough recipes here to restock your entire pantry, start with only two or three favorites to make on a regular basis and rely on the rest to fill in the gaps when you're feeling creative. 🌿

Ingredients You'll Need

With the following nutrient-rich ingredients on hand, you'll be able to make nearly every recipe in this book and bring any meal together in a jiffy. If you are unable to find any of these ingredients locally at a price you're comfortable with, source them online, as many of these ingredients are easy to find. Check out the Appendix at the back of this book if you don't know where to start.

Dairy and Dairy Substitutes

While Chapter 5 includes many recipes for creating your own dairy products, you can certainly purchase them if you prefer. When buying, look for products that come from organic or pastured animals in order to avoid additives and growth hormones.

Milk
Cream
Yogurt
Sour Cream
Butter
Cheese
Almond Milk
Coconut Milk

Meat and Eggs

Choose grass-fed meats and pastured poultry, if possible, when purchasing meats and eggs. Not only will your dollar go farther due to significantly more nutrition in the meat, but you'll also be assured you're supporting sustainable agriculture that treats its animals ethically. Also, when possible, purchase meat still on the bone. Not only is it cheaper, but you can make nutrient-dense stock from the bones after you've eaten the meat, providing excellent nourishment for your body and stretching your food dollars even further.

Ground Beef
Stew Meat
Beef Roast
Sirloin
Pork Chops
Pork Shoulder
Pork Roast
Spiral Ham
Bacon
Chicken (bone-in or whole)
Tuna
Frozen Wild Fish
Shrimp
Eggs

Produce

These common produce items are used frequently throughout this book and having them on hand makes it easy to create your own recipes whenever you feel inspired. Stock your own pantry with your favorite greens, fruits, and vegetables, and buy them fresh each week.

Onions
Garlic
Fresh Ginger
Tomatoes (fresh in season, frozen, or canned)
Lemons
Limes

Nuts and Dried Fruits

These nuts and dried fruits make great additions to granola bars, cereals, and other baking recipes. They also make for easy, portable snacks.

Peanuts
Pistachios
Cashews
Almonds
Pecans
Shredded Coconut
Dried Cranberries
Dried Apricots
Raisins
Dried Figs

Grains and Beans

Beans are a wonderfully healthy and frugal way to eat plenty of protein, minerals, and fiber, and the beans listed here are common ones you're likely to use often.

Grains are likewise very nutritious in their whole form, although there's an increasing number of people today who have difficulty digesting them. Throughout this book, whole wheat and spelt are called for most, but in a few places all-purpose flour is called for, merely to mimic a store-bought texture or flavor as closely as possible.

Grains and beans are frugal and also store well, so they're great to have on hand for emergencies.

All-Purpose Flour (unbleached and unbromated)
Whole-Wheat Flour
Spelt Flour
Buckwheat Flour
Almond Flour

Popcorn
Rolled Oats
Brown Rice
Basmati or Jasmine Rice
Quinoa
Pasta
Kidney Beans
Black Beans
Pinto Beans
Garbanzo Beans
Lentils

Sweeteners and Baking Supplies

Our bodies break every bit of food we eat down into a form of sugar that is usable by our cells. Therefore, our bodies really don't need any extra sugar because it's getting all it needs from the rest of our food. However, when sugar is unrefined, it contains essential minerals and vitamins, and in some cases, like honey, it's got other benefits, like strong antiviral, antibacterial, and antifungal properties. Thus, we need to balance the benefits with the costs–namely, when you eat sweeteners, choose one that still has plenty of vitamins and minerals, but still eat any sweetener in moderation.

Sugar—choose evaporated cane crystals or other whole cane sugar
Raw Honey
Maple Syrup
Blackstrap Molasses
Cocoa Powder
Vanilla Extract (and other flavor extracts)
Starches (like non-GMO cornstarch, arrowroot powder, and tapioca starch)
Baking Powder (aluminum-free)
Baking Soda
Sea Salt (or naturally mined salt)
Vinegars (white, red wine, white wine, malt, and apple cider)

Gelatin

Active Dry Yeast

Herbs and Spices

There are hundreds of delicious, fragrant spices around the world that make great additions to any meal. These are just a few popular ones that will make it easy for you to prepare a variety of meals.

Dried Basil

Bay Leaves

Black Pepper

Black Peppercorns

Cayenne Pepper

Cardamom Pods

Ground Cardamom

Chili Powder

Cinnamon Sticks

Ground Cinnamon

Whole Cloves

Ground Cloves

Cumin

Curry Powder

Dill

Garlic Powder

Ground Ginger

Mustard Powder

Mustard Seeds

Nutmeg (preferably whole)

Minced Onion

Onion Powder

Oregano

Paprika

Parsley

Dried Tarragon

Turmeric

Fats, Oils, and Butters

Healthy fats control sugar cravings, allow all those good vitamins from leafy green vegetables to be assimilated, assure proper cell communication, and support mental focus and acuity. Fats can easily be damaging as well, however, if they have turned rancid, are heavily processed, or are consumed in large quantities, which is why they have gained such a poor reputation in our modern society. The following healthy fats provide a proper balance of saturated and unsaturated fats.

Virgin and Refined Coconut Oil

Butter

Olive Oil

Cocoa Butter

Palm Shortening

Lard, Tallow, and Bacon Grease

Keep in mind that the nutritional data in this book is just a guide and should therefore be taken lightly. Some foods, such as sauerkraut, kimchi, and lox, are preserved using copious amounts of salt, and after fermentation, it's not always possible to determine how much sodium is left in the food. You should always take this into account when selecting recipes, especially if you're on a strict diet, and pay more attention to the quality of your ingredients by selecting whole foods, quality fats, and mineral-rich salts.

Remember, this book is merely a starting place. Make sure to take your preferences and favorite recipes into consideration before stocking your pantry. As you gather new ingredients and your pantry slowly becomes stocked, preparing healthy dinners you love will be that much simpler.

CHAPTER 2

Crackers, Cookies, and Snacks

Snack foods can often be the bane of a person's existence, especially when trying to eat healthy foods bursting with wholesome, all-natural ingredients. Sure, you can munch on carrot sticks, cherry tomatoes, and cheese, but those foods don't always satisfy the cravings that we get. The following recipes will give you the tastes you love without sacrificing your nutrition or filling your body with processed ingredients. They're also great if you're on the road a lot. Whether you're just out running errands or crossing the country on a road trip, these delicious snacks will give you the energy to make it through your day. 🌺

Thin Wheat Crackers

These crackers are crunchy, salty, and surprisingly addictive. The secret to making them is not some magic combination of ingredients, but rather how thin you roll them. You'll want to roll out the dough until it's thinner than a penny, so that the crackers get that crispy, crunchy outside you crave.

HANDS-ON: 25 minutes

INACTIVE: 20 minutes

READY IN: 45 minutes

DIFFICULTY LEVEL: ★ ★

YIELD: Serves 6; Makes 6 dozen crackers

COST PER SERVING: $

CALORIES: 340

FAT: 16 g

PROTEIN: 7 g

SODIUM: 399 mg

FIBER: 6 g

CARBOHYDRATES: 45 g

SUGAR: 9 g

2½ cups whole-wheat or spelt flour

¼ cup sugar or honey

1 teaspoon salt

½ teaspoon paprika

1 teaspoon turmeric

½ teaspoon onion powder

8 tablespoons (1 stick) butter or palm shortening, cubed and very cold

½ cup cold water

Salt, to taste

1. Preheat your oven to 400°F.

2. Lightly grease two baking sheets or line them with parchment paper.

3. Combine the flour, sugar, salt, paprika, turmeric, and onion powder in a medium bowl. Whisk quickly to combine evenly; then drop in the cold butter cubes. Combine the butter with the mixture until the mixture resembles coarse crumbs and holds its shape when squeezed in your hand. Pour in the cold water and mix with wooden spoon until a dough is formed.

4. Scoop the dough into a ball, kneading it once or twice in the bowl. Cover the bowl with plastic wrap or a dish towel and let the dough sit for 5–10 minutes.

5. Divide the dough into two pieces and cover one to keep it from drying out. Dust your work surface liberally with flour and roll the dough as thinly as possible, preferably thinner than a penny. Keep the dough from sticking at all times—feel free to flip, move, and dust the dough as needed.

6. When you've achieved the desired thickness, lift the dough onto the baking sheet. Use a fork to gently poke holes in the dough and sprinkle it with salt. Use a pastry wheel, pizza cutter, or sharp knife to cut the dough into 1½" squares.

7. Set the baking pan in the refrigerator while you roll out the second ball of dough. Place the rolled dough on the remaining baking sheet, repeating all steps and cutting it into squares. Place in the refrigerator.

8. Bake the first sheet of crackers until they are crisp and lightly browned, about 4–7 minutes. Keep a close eye on them, as thin crackers can burn quickly.

9. Remove pan from oven. Let the crackers cool on the pan for 1–2 minutes and then move them to a cooling rack to cool completely.

10. As the first batch cools, bake the second batch of crackers and set them to cool.

11. Store the crackers in an airtight container for up to 2 weeks.

DIFFERENT FLAVOR VARIATION

For a "Garden Vegetable" version of these crackers, grind together 2 tablespoons dehydrated bell peppers, 1 tablespoon onion powder, 1 tablespoon finely chopped sun-dried tomatoes, 1 teaspoon celery seed, and 1 teaspoon garlic powder in a spice grinder until finely ground. Add this mixture to the dry ingredients in Step 3 of the above recipe. You may need to add 1 extra tablespoon of water if your dough is too dry.

Cheddar Cheese Crackers

These crackers are the best of two worlds—the savory decadence of a yeast cracker with the speed of preparation of a quick-dough cracker. The turmeric in this recipe adds a warm, yellow hue to the crackers, but if you don't have it, they'll turn out just as delicious, only lighter in color.

HANDS-ON: 30 minutes

INACTIVE: 15 minutes

READY IN: 45 minutes

DIFFICULTY LEVEL:
★ ★ ★ ★

YIELD: Serves 8; Makes 10 dozen crackers

COST PER SERVING: $ $

CALORIES: 170

FAT: 8 g

PROTEIN: 5 g

SODIUM: 333 mg

FIBER: 1 g

CARBOHYDRATES: 19 g

SUGAR: 0 g

½ cup tepid water
1 teaspoon active dry yeast
1½ cups all-purpose flour
½ teaspoon salt
½ teaspoon baking soda
2 teaspoons nutritional yeast
1 teaspoon onion powder
1 teaspoon mustard powder
1 teaspoon turmeric (optional)
2 ounces (¾ cup loosely packed) shredded Cheddar cheese
¼ cup butter or vegetable shortening, cut into pieces and chilled

1. Preheat the oven to 350°F and line two large baking sheets with parchment paper.

2. Place the water in a small bowl and stir in the active dry yeast until it's dissolved. Set the bowl aside, uncovered, for about 5 minutes.

3. Place the flour, salt, baking soda, nutritional yeast, onion powder, mustard powder, and turmeric in a food processor and pulse until combined. Add the cheese and cold butter cubes; then pulse until the mixture resembles the texture of fine crumbs.

4. Drizzle in the water and yeast mixture, pulsing or stirring until the dough is shaggy, or until all the ingredients have been incorporated, Gather it together on a lightly floured work surface and knead until cohesive, about 1 minute.

5. Divide the dough into two balls. Flatten one ball to about 1" thick; then cover it with plastic wrap and place it in the refrigerator. On a lightly floured surface, roll out the other ball of dough until it's very thin, about ⅟₁₆" thick. As you roll, make sure the dough isn't sticking to the work surface, flouring the surface and your rolling pin as necessary.

6. Cut the dough into a rectangle; then transfer it to the prepared baking sheet. Prick the dough all over with a fork about 1" apart and cut it into 1½" squares with a pizza cutter or sharp knife. Set aside (in the refrigerator, if possible) and remove the reserved disk of dough from the refrigerator. Repeat all steps with the second batch of dough.

7. Bake both sheets of crackers, rotating the baking sheets if necessary, for about 13–16 minutes. They should be firm, dry, and just beginning to brown on the bottom. Keep a close eye on the crackers toward the end of the baking time, as thin crackers can burn quickly.

8. Remove pan from oven and place crackers on a cooling rack. Cool completely before storing them in an airtight container for up to 1 week.

Graham Crackers

There isn't anything else quite like homemade graham crackers. They're flaky, light, and filled with just the perfect combination of flavors. This recipe uses two popular pastry techniques to create the texture and taste we've loved for all these years. The two keys here are cutting in the butter only until the lumps are the size of very coarse crumbs (rather than going all the way to fine crumbs) and keeping the dough absolutely cold, which gives the cracker its layers as it bakes.

HANDS-ON: 30 minutes

INACTIVE: 3 hours

READY IN: 3½ hours

DIFFICULTY LEVEL:
★ ★ ★ ★

YIELD: Serves 10; Makes 20 graham crackers

COST PER SERVING: $ $

CALORIES: 267

FAT: 10 g

PROTEIN: 4 g

SODIUM: 368 mg

FIBER: 4 g

CARBOHYDRATES: 42 g

SUGAR: 20 g

2½ cups whole-wheat flour

½ cup whole cane sugar

1 teaspoon baking soda

1 teaspoon sea salt

4 ounces butter (8 tablespoons/1 stick), cut into ½" cubes and chilled

⅓ cup honey

¼ cup milk

2 tablespoons vanilla extract

1. Preheat the oven to 350°F.

2. Place the flour, sugar, baking soda, and salt in a large bowl and whisk to combine. Add the cold butter cubes and combine with the flour mixture until the mixture is the texture of very coarse crumbs and holds together loosely when pressed into your hand.

3. Add the honey, milk, and vanilla extract and mix until the dough just comes together. It should be very soft and sticky. Place the dough on a large piece of parchment paper and cover it with a second piece of parchment paper. Press down on the dough until it is about 1" thick. Place the covered dough in the refrigerator and chill until firm, at least 2 hours.

4. When the dough is firm, divide it in half and return one half to the refrigerator. Lightly flour your work surface and roll the dough into a long rectangle about ⅛" thick. Since it is sticky, make sure you dust your work surface and rolling pin with flour as necessary.

5. When the dough is ⅛" thick, cut it into 1½" squares using a cookie cutter, pizza roller, or sharp knife. Place the graham crackers on a parchment paper– or silicone-lined baking sheet.

6. Roll out the second batch of dough and repeat Steps 4 and 5. Add the new batch of crackers to the baking sheet (or start a new one, if necessary). Cover with a tea towel and chill until firm, at least 30 minutes.

7. Prick each cracker several times with a fork. If you have cut traditional rectangular crackers, score one vertical and one horizontal line on the cracker, as well. These holes help the cracker bake correctly, so they're not just for decoration.

8. Bake for 20–25 minutes, until browned and slightly firm to the touch, rotating the sheet(s) halfway through to ensure even baking. Start checking the crackers after 15 minutes, as crackers can burn quickly.

9. Cool the crackers on the baking sheet for about 5 minutes, and then transfer them to a cooling rack to cool completely. Store crackers in an airtight container for up to 1 week.

Fruit Roll-Ups

Homemade fruit leather is notorious for ending up extremely chewy or brittle due to over-drying. By adding yogurt, you not only get the benefits of the probiotics; you also soften the leather and make it a bit more manageable.

HANDS-ON: 10 minutes

INACTIVE: 4–12 hours

READY IN: 12 hours

DIFFICULTY LEVEL: ★ ★ ★

YIELD: Serves 16; Makes 16 roll-ups

COST PER SERVING: $ $

GF

CALORIES: 62

FAT: 1 g

PROTEIN: 1 g

SODIUM: 15 mg

FIBER: 0 g

CARBOHYDRATES: 13 g

SUGAR: 12 g

2 cups fresh or frozen soft fruit (berries, peaches, apricots, cherries, etc.)

2 cups yogurt

2 teaspoons lemon juice

1 teaspoon vanilla extract

½ cup honey or maple syrup

Sprinkle of cinnamon (optional)

1. If using an oven to dehydrate the leathers, preheat it to 140°F.

2. Place all ingredients in a blender or food processor and blend until smooth. If the mixture gets foamy, set aside for a minute or two to let the bubbles subside. If you want a seedless leather, pass the purée through a fine-mesh sieve.

3. To dehydrate the fruit mixture in your oven, line the bottom of a large baking sheet with parchment paper and pour the purée onto the paper. The purée should be about ¹⁄₁₆" thick, and there should be a 1" border around the edge of the paper. Place the purée in the oven and cook until completely dry, about 8–12 hours.

4. If you're dehydrating your leather in a food dehydrator, line a few dehydrator trays with parchment paper. Pour the purée onto the parchment paper and spread thin, preferably about ¹⁄₁₆" thick and leaving a 1" border around the edge. Dehydrate at 140°F for 4–8 hours.

5. The fruit leather is done when it is no longer sticky to the touch and the edge easily lifts up from the parchment paper. Roll the parchment paper into a tightly rolled tube, preferably while still warm, and slice or snip it into 1" strips.

6. Once cool, store the fruit leather in an airtight container for up to 3 weeks.

Chewy Fruit Snacks

Fruit snacks are great anytime snacks because they can go anywhere. Whether you're packing a child's lunch, needing something to tide you over during an afternoon slump, or wanting a quick burst of energy when you're out on a trail, these fruit snacks are certainly one of the best treats to have on hand. Due to the high percentage of gelatin, they're firm enough to put up with travel and also provide you a good dose of protein. For the best flavor, choose very full-flavored fruits and fruit juices, such as berries, cherries, pomegranates, or blueberries.

HANDS-ON: 10 minutes

INACTIVE: 2–3 hours

READY IN: 3 hours

DIFFICULTY LEVEL: ★ ★

YIELD: Serves 6; Makes 144 fruit snacks

COST PER SERVING: $ $

CALORIES: 111

FAT: 0 g

PROTEIN: 6 g

SODIUM: 16 mg

FIBER: 1 g

CARBOHYDRATES: 25 g

SUGAR: 20 g

1 cup puréed fruit
1 cup strongly flavored fruit juice
¼ cup honey
1 cup cold water
⅓ cup (about 8 packets) unflavored gelatin

1. Place fruit in a blender and purée until smooth. Make sure the final puréed product is equal to 1 cup.

2. Add the fruit juice and honey to the blender and purée again until smooth. Pour mixture into a large bowl and set aside. Have a whisk or a large spoon at the ready.

3. Fill a saucepan with 1 cup cold water and stir in the gelatin until combined. The mixture will be very thick and will want to congeal.

4. Place over medium-low heat and heat the mixture until the gelatin is dissolved, stirring occasionally, 3–4 minutes. With this amount of gelatin, it can sometimes be difficult to see whether all the gelatin is dissolved, but you'll be able to make an educated guess by stirring it gently and observing whether whole granules are moving around in the mixture or not.

5. Pour the dissolved gelatin into the fruit mixture and whisk well to combine. Quickly pour the mixture into an ungreased 9" × 9" cake pan or into candy molds and allow to cool in the refrigerator uncovered for 2–3 hours. If you're using candy molds, know that you must work extremely fast or the mix will set before you can pour it all.

6. Allow the fruit snacks to set completely before removing them from the cake pan or molds. If using a cake pan, place the fruit snack mixture on a cutting board and cut it into 144 pieces by cutting 12 strips, then cutting each strip into 12 pieces.

7. Store in an airtight container at room temperature for 2–3 days, or in the refrigerator for 1–2 weeks.

Black-and-White Sandwich Cookies

Who doesn't love indulging in this classic snack? While such guilty pleasures certainly are delightful, the store-bought versions of these popular sandwich cookies are filled with artificial ingredients, chemically refined flours, and high fructose corn syrup. This homemade recipe takes that ubiquitous childhood snack and turns it into delicious cookies that you don't have to feel bad about eating! Also, if you make your own powdered sugar (see the recipe in Chapter 7), you'll be using a less refined sugar, which at least provides a few minerals in your sugary indulgence.

HANDS-ON: 30 minutes

INACTIVE: 2 hours

READY IN: 2½ hours

DIFFICULTY LEVEL: ★ ★

YIELD: Serves 10; Makes 20 sandwich cookies

COST PER SERVING: $ $ $

CALORIES: 309

FAT: 18 g

PROTEIN: 4 g

SODIUM: 254 mg

FIBER: 3 g

CARBOHYDRATES: 38 g

SUGAR: 24 g

FOR THE COOKIE WAFERS:

1¼ cups whole-wheat or spelt flour

½ cup unsweetened cocoa powder

1 teaspoon baking soda

½ teaspoon sea salt

10 tablespoons (1¼ sticks) unsalted butter or coconut oil, softened

1 cup unrefined cane sugar

1 large egg

3–4 teaspoons chocolate extract (optional)

FOR THE FILLING:

¼ cup palm shortening

⅓ cup powdered sugar

1. Preheat the oven to 375°F. Lightly grease a baking sheet or line it with parchment paper.

2. In a medium bowl, stir the flour, cocoa powder, baking soda, and salt together with a whisk. Set aside.

3. In a large bowl, cream the butter and the sugar together with an electric mixer on high until fluffy. Reduce the speed to medium-low and add in the egg and the chocolate extract.

4. Reduce the speed again to low and add in the dry ingredients, one spoonful at a time. Mix until the dough is completely mixed.

5. Roll the dough into ¾" balls and place on the prepared baking sheet approximately 2" apart. Flatten each ball to a ⅛"-thick disk. If you want to be really fancy, you can use an old-fashioned shortbread cookie stamp.

6. Bake for 8–9 minutes, rotating once for even baking.

7. Let the cookies cool on the baking sheet for about 5 minutes before removing them to a cooling rack.

8. While the cookies are cooling, create the filling by creaming the shortening and powdered sugar with an electric mixer on medium-high until very smooth. Set aside at room temperature.

9. Once the cookies have cooled completely, flip half of them upside down so their bottom side is facing up. Spoon a dollop of filling onto each upside-down cookie. Press the remaining cookies onto the cookies topped with filling. The filling should reach the outer edge of the cookies.

10. For the best taste and texture, place cookies in the refrigerator for at least 1 hour before serving.

11. Store in an airtight container in the refrigerator for up to 1 week, or in the freezer for up to 3 months.

Potato Chips

Potato chips are a delightful treat, and making them in the oven makes the task quicker and far less messy than their deep-fried counterparts. Keep in mind that the thickness of the slices in this recipe makes a big difference. If you make them too thin, the edges will burn before the middle is done, and if you slice them too thick, then the entire outside will crust over while leaving the insides soft. The perfect slice is an even 1/16" thickness, which is about the thickness of a penny. However, don't despair—even if you can't get perfect slices, just keep an eye on them while they're in the oven to keep them from getting too crisp.

HANDS-ON: 15 minutes

INACTIVE: 30 minutes

READY IN: 45 minutes

DIFFICULTY LEVEL: ★ ★

YIELD: Serves 4; Makes 4 cups

COST PER SERVING: $

CALORIES: 188

FAT: 7 g

PROTEIN: 3 g

SODIUM: 601 mg

FIBER: 5 g

CARBOHYDRATES: 29 g

SUGAR: 2 g

2 whole firm-fleshed potatoes (i.e. Sieglinde, Yukon gold, or New potatoes)

2 tablespoons olive oil

1 teaspoon sea salt

½ teaspoon black pepper

¼ teaspoon smoked paprika

1. Preheat the oven to 400°F and line a large baking sheet with parchment paper.

2. Wash and dry the potatoes. Slice them thin, about the thickness of a penny, using a mandoline or knife.

3. Place the potato slices in a large bowl and drizzle olive oil over them. Toss the slices to coat them evenly.

4. Lay the potato slices out in an even layer on the baking sheet. Bake them until they're a deep, golden brown but not burned, about 25–30 minutes. Remove the chips from the baking sheet and let sit until they cool completely. They will finish crisping as they sit, so resist the urge to return them to the oven.

5. Sprinkle the chips with salt, pepper, and paprika, and serve.

6. Store in an airtight container for 1–2 days.

Granola Bars

At the grocery store, you'll find shelf after shelf of granola bars, but most of these treats aren't as healthy as their boxes say they are. Using barley malt syrup in this recipe gives the bars a nutty flavor that is difficult to resist but also cuts down on the sugar, so they're not quite as sweet—or bad for you—as the store-bought variety. To pack these up for the road, just wrap them in wax paper or place them in a resealable container before heading out the door.

HANDS-ON: 15 minutes

INACTIVE: 1 hour 45 minutes

READY IN: 2 hours

DIFFICULTY LEVEL: ★ ★

YIELD: Serves 12; Makes 24 bars

COST PER SERVING: $ $

CALORIES: 248

FAT: 16 g

PROTEIN: 6 g

SODIUM: 200 mg

FIBER: 3 g

CARBOHYDRATES: 22 g

SUGAR: 9 g

2 cups oats, divided

2 cups add-ins (sunflower seeds, flax meal, chopped nuts, flaked coconut, etc.)

⅓ cup maple syrup or barley malt syrup

3 tablespoons unrefined cane sugar

1 teaspoon sea salt

⅓ cup coconut oil or butter

1. Preheat oven to 300°F. Line a baking sheet with parchment paper and set aside.

2. In a large mixing bowl, pour in 1½ cups of the oats. Add the other ½ cup of oats to a blender and pulse for about 45 seconds, until the oats have been pulverized into flour. Add the oat flour to the large mixing bowl. Mix in whichever nuts, seeds, or other add-ins you desire.

3. In a large, heavy-bottomed saucepan, heat the maple syrup, sugar, salt, and coconut oil over medium heat, just until the sugar is completely dissolved, 2–3 minutes.

4. Pour the syrup mixture over the oat mixture and stir to coat completely.

5. Using a well-oiled spatula, scrape the oat mixture onto the prepared parchment paper and press the oats down as compactly as possible, preferably until about ¼" thick.

6. Bake for 35 minutes, until a deep golden, or 25–30 minutes, if you like softer bars.

7. Cool the mixture for about 10 minutes and then cut it into 24 bars without removing from the baking sheet. Let the bars sit for 1 hour. Once set, cut them again with a sharp knife and lift them off the pan.

8. Store in an airtight container for up to 2 weeks, or in the freezer for up to 6 months.

French Onion Chip Dip

This quick dip is perfect for parties and unexpected guests! If you have more than 30 minutes to spare, you can make a killer version of this recipe by stirring a caramelized onion into this mix instead of the dry onion flakes. However, if you just found out that you've got guests arriving in less than 10 minutes, this quick chip dip is your go-to, especially if you have the Dry Onion Soup Mix (see recipe in Chapter 4) on hand. Using the mix will help you get this dip out to guests in about 2 minutes flat!

HANDS-ON: 5 minutes

INACTIVE: none

READY IN: 5 minutes

DIFFICULTY LEVEL: ★

YIELD: Serves 8; Makes 2¼ cups

COST PER SERVING: $

CALORIES: 114

FAT: 11 g

PROTEIN: 1 g

SODIUM: 268 mg

FIBER: 0 g

CARBOHYDRATES: 2 g

SUGAR: 2 g

2 cups sour cream

3 tablespoons dried onion flakes

1 teaspoon onion powder

1 teaspoon parsley flakes

½ teaspoon celery seed

¾ teaspoon salt

⅛ teaspoon ground black pepper

Dash Worcestershire sauce (optional)

1. Whisk ingredients together in a small bowl.

2. For the best results, chill mixture in the refrigerator for at least 30 minutes before serving. You can also serve this dip to guests immediately, if pressed for time. Store in an airtight container in the refrigerator for up to 5 days.

Jerky

Jerky is an easy food to grab when you're on the go. Loaded with flavor and healthy ingredients, this snack is great for trail days, or just when you need an energy boost throughout your day. If you're vegan, replace the meat with large shiitake or portabella mushroom caps and skip the honey. Keep in mind, though, that you'll need to cut the dehydrating time in half and there's no need to do the final heating step in the oven since the final heating step is just to make sure that any harmful bacteria in the meat is sufficiently destroyed.

HANDS-ON: 20 minutes

INACTIVE: 24 hours

READY IN: 24 hours

DIFFICULTY LEVEL: ★ ★

YIELD: Serves 12; Makes 1 pound

COST PER SERVING: $ $ $

CALORIES: 229

FAT: 8 g

PROTEIN: 25 g

SODIUM: 312 mg

FIBER: 0 g

CARBOHYDRATES: 13 g

SUGAR: 9 g

3 pounds beef brisket or flank steak

1 cup Worcestershire sauce

1 cup traditionally fermented soy sauce

¼ cup honey

6 cloves garlic, minced

½ medium white or yellow onion, minced

½ teaspoon black pepper

2 teaspoons liquid smoke

1. If using an oven to dehydrate the meat, preheat it to 150°F.

2. Freeze the brisket for 15–20 minutes. Once frozen, slice it very thinly against the grain, about the thickness of a penny. Remove any visible fat.

3. Combine remaining ingredients in a large bowl or large resealable plastic bag. Add sliced meat and stir or shake to coat evenly. Refrigerate for 8–12 hours, turning or stirring every few hours.

4. Remove the meat from the marinade and blot dry with a paper towel. You'll want to get the meat as dry as possible. Discard marinade.

5. To dehydrate the meat in your oven, cover the bottom of the oven with aluminum foil and place the strips of meat directly on the oven racks. Dry for about 4–8 hours.

6. If you're dehydrating your meat in a food dehydrator, place the strips of meat on the trays, making sure that they do not overlap. Parchment paper can be helpful, as these will drip as they dry, but you may want to flip the jerky half-way through so that the bottom dries completely. Dehydrate the meat at 150°F for 4–8 hours.

7. The meat is done when it is very firm and dry, but also still pliable. It shouldn't break when bent. Once dehydrated, turn the oven to 300°F and place your jerky directly on the racks and bake for 10 minutes to kill any harmful bacteria. Remove it from the oven and let it cool completely.

8. Store in an airtight container for 1–2 months, or for up to 6 months in the freezer.

CHAPTER 3

Breads and Cereals

Since cereals and breads are one of the most processed foods on the market, they are one of the most challenging foods to replicate in a home kitchen. The shapes and textures we know and love as part of our morning breakfast routines have been created from machines that mash, extrude, and cook grains in such extreme ways and at such extreme temperatures that they no longer resemble the wholesome ingredients from nature. While cornflakes and white bread may be too commercial to make at home, nugget-style cereals and a variety of artisan breads can easily be made using everyday ingredients and will provide you with the full spectrum of nutrition grains can provide. 🌿

Hamburger and Hot Dog Buns

These hamburger and hot dog buns are sure to be a hit at your next picnic or barbecue. They're soft, delicious, and best of all—free from the dough enhancers and additives commercial bread companies use to extend the shelf life of their products. Also, a tip: bread dough textures can vary significantly according to your brand of flour, the type of flour, your climate, and other factors, so if you have a scale, weigh all your ingredients the first time you make this recipe and you'll be able to more easily replicate your scrumptious results every time you make these buns.

HANDS-ON: 25 minutes

INACTIVE: 3 hours

READY IN: 3½ hours

DIFFICULTY LEVEL: ★ ★

YIELD: Serves 12; Makes 12 hamburger or hot dog buns

COST PER SERVING: $

CALORIES: 300

FAT: 12 g

PROTEIN: 10 g

SODIUM: 312 mg

FIBER: 7 g

CARBOHYDRATES: 44 g

SUGAR: 3 g

½ cup, plus ⅞ cup lukewarm water, divided

2 tablespoons honey

2 tablespoons active dry yeast

5½ cups whole-wheat, spelt, or all-purpose flour, divided

1½ teaspoons salt

2 teaspoons onion powder (optional)

8 tablespoons softened butter

2 eggs

1 teaspoon red wine vinegar

4 tablespoons melted butter, for brushing

1. Place ½ cup of water in a medium bowl and stir in honey until dissolved. Sprinkle the yeast over the water mixture and let sit until bubbly, about 5 minutes.

2. Add 3 cups of flour as well as the salt, onion powder (if using), butter, eggs, vinegar, and the remaining water. Combine using the paddle attachment on an electric mixer. Once everything is incorporated, turn the mixer to high and beat the dough for about 2 minutes. Switch to the dough hook and stir in the remaining flour on low.

3. Once all the flour is incorporated, turn the mixer to medium-high and knead the dough for another 2–3 minutes. Add water or flour as needed, 1 tablespoon at a time. The end result should be soft but not sticky.

4. Place the dough in a lightly greased bowl and cover with a tea towel. Let the dough rise until it's puffy, about 1 hour.

5. Scrape the dough onto your work counter and divide it into twelve pieces.

6. To make hamburger buns, shape the dough into balls and place them on an unfloured surface. Cup your hand over each ball and twist

gently counterclockwise. Place the balls on a parchment paper–lined baking sheet and gently flatten each piece until it's about 4" wide.

7. To make hot dog buns, shape the buns into oblong, oval-shaped balls and press down in the middle with the side of your hand to create an indentation. Pull the sides of the dough up and set aside on the baking sheet.

8. Cover the dough on baking sheet with a tea towel and let it rise for another 1–1½ hours, until puffy.

9. Preheat the oven to 350°F. Brush each bun with melted butter.

10. Bake until the buns are just beginning to brown, 20–22 minutes.

11. Remove the buns from the oven, transfer to a rack, and brush with the remaining melted butter.

12. Allow the buns to cool completely. Store in an airtight container at room temperature for up to 3 days.

Whole Grain Nugget Cereal

This is another great recipe for all those days you're craving an easy, filling breakfast free of overly refined grains. The bite-size pieces will give you that crunch that makes nugget-style cereals so great, and the barley malt syrup in this recipe gives you that nutty, malty flavor that you'll find in your favorite name brands.

HANDS-ON: 15 minutes

INACTIVE: 2¾ hours

READY IN: 3 hours

DIFFICULTY LEVEL: ★ ★

YIELD: Serves 12; Makes 6 cups

COST PER SERVING: $ $

CALORIES: 193

FAT: 1 g

PROTEIN: 7 g

SODIUM: 337 mg

FIBER: 5 g

CARBOHYDRATES: 42 g

SUGAR: 7 g

1½ cups buttermilk, or 1⅓ cups milk plus 3 tablespoons lemon juice

3¾ cups whole-wheat, spelt, graham, barley, and/or sprouted wheat flour

⅔ cup barley malt syrup

¼ cup honey or maple syrup

1 teaspoon molasses (optional)

1 teaspoon sea salt

1 teaspoon baking soda

1. Preheat oven to 375°F.

2. If using milk and lemon juice, stir together and let mixture sit for 5 minutes to thicken.

3. Mix all ingredients together with an electric mixer until smooth. Add a few more tablespoons of buttermilk if the mixture is crumbly.

4. Scrape dough onto a parchment paper– or silicone-lined baking sheet. With well-greased hands, press the dough into all corners of the sheet. Bake for 15–20 minutes, or until a toothpick comes out clean. Cool completely.

5. Once cool, preheat the oven to 200°F and break the bread into large pieces. Pulse in a food processor until the pieces are bite-size.

6. Return pieces to baking sheet or a large sheet cake pan. Bake for 1½–2 hours, or until very crisp and just slightly brown. Make sure to stir the pieces every 15 minutes to ensure even crisping.

7. Cool completely and store in an airtight container for up to 1 month.

Almond Peanut Butter Breakfast Cereal

This grain-free cereal is popular with kids and adults alike and is sure to be a new favorite in your breakfast and snack line-up. And a word to the wise: to get the best crunch, the best "last-ability" in milk, and the best flavor, bake the crumbs for as long as you can without over-browning them. The toasted nut flavor is irresistible.

HANDS-ON: 15 minutes

INACTIVE: 3¾ hours

READY IN: 4 hours

DIFFICULTY LEVEL: ★ ★

YIELD: Serves 12; Makes 6 cups

COST PER SERVING: $ $ $

GF V EF

CALORIES: 371

FAT: 29 g

PROTEIN: 11 g

SODIUM: 335 mg

FIBER: 4 g

CARBOHYDRATES: 22 g

SUGAR: 16 g

1½ cups buttermilk, or 1⅓ cups milk plus 3 tablespoons lemon juice

2½ cups almond flour or almond meal

1 cup peanut butter

⅓ cup coconut oil, melted

½ cup honey

½ teaspoon sea salt

1 teaspoon baking soda

1 teaspoon vanilla extract

1. Preheat oven to 325°F.

2. If using milk and lemon juice, stir together and let the mixture sit for 5 minutes to thicken.

3. Mix all ingredients together with an electric mixer until smooth. Add a few more tablespoons of buttermilk if the mixture is crumbly.

4. Spread dough onto a parchment paper– or silicone-lined baking sheet. Bake for 30–35 minutes, or until the edges are well browned and the entire top is dry to the touch. The inside may still be soft. Cool completely.

5. Once cool, preheat the oven to 250°F and tear the almond bread into large pieces. Pulse in a food processor until the pieces are bite-size.

6. Return crumbs to baking sheet or a large sheet cake pan. Bake for 2–3 hours, or until very crisp and slightly brown. Make sure to stir the pieces every 15 minutes to ensure even crisping.

7. Cool completely and store in an airtight container for up to 1 month.

Granola

Ah, granola, the ubiquitous health cereal. Some traditionalists say oats aren't healthy unless you soak and dry them first, but honestly, this is a far-cry healthier than the expensive boxes you buy in the store with processed sugars and preservatives. This slightly sweet version has a perky secret ingredient that will satisfy every time and leave you wanting more (and no, it's not MSG).

HANDS-ON: 15 minutes	
INACTIVE: 1 hour 45 minutes	
READY IN: 2 hours	
DIFFICULTY LEVEL: ★ ★	
YIELD: Serves 24; Makes 12 cups	
COST PER SERVING: $ $	

CALORIES: 224

FAT: 12 g

PROTEIN: 5 g

SODIUM: 53 mg

FIBER: 4 g

CARBOHYDRATES: 26 g

SUGAR: 10 g

⅓ cup maple syrup

⅓ cup unrefined cane sugar

1 tablespoon vanilla extract

½ cup melted butter or coconut oil

½ teaspoon salt

¼ teaspoon black pepper

5 cups oats

3 cups chopped nuts and seeds (pecans, almonds, sunflower seeds, pumpkin seeds, etc.)

2 cups dried fruit (raisins, cranberries, apricots, cherries, currants, etc.)

1. Preheat the oven to 325°F.

2. Whisk the maple syrup, sugar, vanilla, butter, salt, and pepper in a large bowl.

3. Stir in the oats, nuts, and seeds and mix until everything is well coated in the liquid mixture.

4. Spread on a parchment paper–lined baking sheet and press down firmly to create a thin layer.

5. Bake for 30–35 minutes, turning the baking sheet once if necessary to bake evenly. Remove from the oven when the granola is golden and press down on the mixture lightly with a spatula once again.

6. Let it cool in the pan for 1 hour. Break the hardened mixture into pieces and stir in the dried fruit.

7. Store in an airtight container for up to 2 weeks.

Cornbread

For many, cornbread is the ultimate comfort food and goes well with just about anything, including chili, chowder, and barbecue. This recipe is so easy that you'll have it memorized in no time! You can also turn it into a mix to store for later use by just combining the first five ingredients and storing the mix in an airtight container for up to 6 months.

HANDS-ON: 10 minutes

INACTIVE: 20 minutes

READY IN: 30 minutes

DIFFICULTY LEVEL: ★

YIELD: Serves 4; Makes 8 wedges or 9 squares

COST PER SERVING: $

CALORIES: 466

FAT: 17 g

PROTEIN: 11 g

SODIUM: 656 mg

FIBER: 2 g

CARBOHYDRATES: 68 g

SUGAR: 17 g

1 cup all-purpose flour

1 cup cornmeal

4 tablespoons sugar

1 tablespoon baking powder

1 teaspoon salt

2 eggs

1 cup milk

¼ cup melted butter

1. Preheat the oven to 375°F. Grease a 9" × 9" pan or a deep dish pie pan with butter.

2. Whisk together the flour, cornmeal, sugar, baking powder, and salt in a large bowl.

3. Make a well in the middle of the dry ingredients and crack the eggs in. Whisk them lightly. Add in the milk and the melted butter; then stir until combined. There should be no lumps.

4. Pour the batter into the prepared dish and bake for 18–22 minutes, or until the top is just beginning to brown and a toothpick inserted in the center comes out clean.

5. Store in an airtight container at room temperature for up to 2 days.

Honey Whole-Wheat No Knead Bread

The secret to this bread is not the exact quantities of the ingredients, although they definitely determine its rise and density. The secret to a good, satisfying loaf is the pan. Any solid, thick-walled Dutch oven with a lid will work, but a cast-iron one works wonders. Make sure to do the full preheat to bring the pan to temperature. Feel free to experiment with the flours and additives, like dried fruit and chocolate chips, to add your own touch to this recipe.

HANDS-ON: 5 minutes

INACTIVE: 8–21 hours

READY IN: 21 hours

DIFFICULTY LEVEL: ★

YIELD: Serves 4; Makes 1 loaf

COST PER SERVING: $

CALORIES: 338

FAT: 2 g

PROTEIN: 12 g

SODIUM: 1,037 mg

FIBER: 11 g

CARBOHYDRATES: 74 g

SUGAR: 9 g

1⅝ cups warm water

2 tablespoons honey

3 cups whole-wheat or spelt flour

¼ teaspoon active dry yeast

1¾ teaspoons salt

1. Pour the warm water into a measuring cup and stir in the honey until it dissolves. Set aside.

2. In a large bowl, combine flour, yeast, and salt. Whisk once or twice to combine well. Pour the warm honeyed water over the flour and stir until blended. The dough will be very wet and shaggy.

3. Cover with a dish towel and set aside undisturbed at room temperature (68–72°F) for 6–18 hours. The dough will be ready to bake at any time during this period. (This is what makes it an extremely versatile bread.) When the dough is ready, the surface will be covered with little bubbles and the dough will be very soft but not liquid.

4. Scrape the dough onto a well-floured surface. Toss the dough back and forth lightly on the work surface with your fingertips 4–5 times. Cover it with plastic wrap, a well-floured dish towel, or an inverted mixing bowl and let the dough rest for 2 hours.

5. Preheat to 450°F 3-quart (or larger) Dutch oven in the oven.

6. Once the oven has been preheated for at least 30 minutes, remove the Dutch oven from the oven and quickly transfer the dough into it, trying to make any seam land side up. (If it doesn't, don't stress. It's perfectly okay if it looks messy.)

7. Cover with the lid and bake for 30–35 minutes. If the top is not a golden brown, bake without the lid for another 5 minutes.

8. Shake the bread loose from the pan and onto a cooling rack. Serve when it has cooled completely or store in an airtight container for up to 3 days.

Biscuits

Biscuits are the perfect accompaniment to nearly any meal—a side to roasted chicken and corn-on-the-cob, a base for biscuits and gravy, or a snack to take to the park. If you've never made flaky, homemade biscuits before, you're in for a treat!

HANDS-ON: 15 minutes

INACTIVE: 15 minutes

READY IN: 30 minutes

DIFFICULTY LEVEL: ★ ★

YIELD: Serves 6; Makes 12 biscuits

COST PER SERVING: $

CALORIES: 410

FAT: 17 g

PROTEIN: 8 g

SODIUM: 420 mg

FIBER: 2 g

CARBOHYDRATES: 57 g

SUGAR: 8 g

3 cups all-purpose flour

2½ tablespoons sugar or honey

1½ tablespoons baking powder

1 teaspoon sea salt

8 tablespoons (1 stick) cold butter, cubed

⅔ cup buttermilk or ⅔ cup milk + 2 tablespoons lemon juice

½ cup whole milk

1. Preheat the oven to 400°F.

2. Sift or whisk together the flour, sugar, baking powder, and salt. If you're using honey instead of sugar, add it later by drizzling it into the dough when you add the milks.

3. Combine the butter with the flour mixture until it forms pea-size pieces and loosely holds together when pressed in your hand. Add the buttermilk and whole milk. Mix just to combine the ingredients— don't overmix.

4. Roll the dough out to a 1" thickness; then fold in half, roll, fold in half, and repeat three or four times for a final thickness of 1". (This process of laminating the dough ensures fluffy, flaky biscuits.) Cut the dough into rounds with a biscuit cutter and place the rounds on an ungreased baking sheet.

5. Bake until golden brown, 10–15 minutes. Serve hot or let cool on wire racks, then store in an airtight container for up to 3 days.

Pizza Crust

This is a fantastic, reliable, everyday pizza dough. The advantage to making crusts ahead of time is that when you're craving pizza or just want a quick meal at the end of a long day, you don't have to rely on take-out or store-bought frozen pizzas; you can easily take a crust out of the freezer, throw on some simple toppings, and bake. In fact, if you're really pressed for time, you can just bake one of these crusts as is, cut it into breadsticks, and dip it in your favorite Pasta Sauce (see Chapter 7). Paired with a good salad, it makes a simple yet elegant meal.

HANDS-ON: 20 minutes

INACTIVE: 1 hour

READY IN: 1½ hours

DIFFICULTY LEVEL: ★

YIELD: Serves 8; Makes 4 12" pizza crusts

COST PER SERVING: $

CALORIES: 435

FAT: 9 g

PROTEIN: 15 g

SODIUM: 891 mg

FIBER: 13 g

CARBOHYDRATES: 80 g

SUGAR: 4 g

2½ cups lukewarm water

4½ teaspoons (2 packages) active dry yeast

1 tablespoon salt

2 tablespoons sugar

4 tablespoons extra-virgin olive oil

7 cups all-purpose, spelt, or whole-wheat flour

1. Pour the water into a medium bowl or the bowl of an electric mixer and stir in the yeast until it dissolves. Let it sit until bubbly, about 5 minutes.

2. Add the salt, sugar, and olive oil and begin to mix on slow. Add the flour 1 spoonful at a time until all 7 cups of flour have been added. Continue to mix the dough until it is smooth and springy, 5–7 minutes.

3. Cover the bowl with a damp cloth and let rise until the dough has doubled in size, about 1 hour.

4. Punch down the dough and divide it into four pieces. Roll each piece to about ¼" thick and separate them with pieces of parchment paper. Wrap the bunch together in foil and place them in the freezer for up to 3 months.

5. When you are ready to bake, just take a crust out of the freezer, top with your favorite toppings, and bake at 400°F for 18–22 minutes.

Flour Tortillas

These Tex-Mex style tortillas are addictively good. Being a flour tortilla (as opposed to corn), they're not necessarily authentic south of the border, but they are still the perfect companion for your favorite fajitas, tacos, and refried beans. They also work well as an all-natural, generic flatbread. Use these any time you need a soft wrap to go with gyros, falafels, or hummus. They're extremely versatile.

HANDS-ON: 25 minutes

INACTIVE: 30 minutes–12 hours

READY IN: 1 hour

DIFFICULTY LEVEL: ★ ★

YIELD: Serves 4; Makes 1 dozen tortillas

COST PER SERVING: $

CALORIES: 367

FAT: 4 g

PROTEIN: 10 g

SODIUM: 1,008 mg

FIBER: 3 g

CARBOHYDRATES: 72 g

SUGAR: 0 g

---

3 cups all-purpose flour

1 teaspoon baking powder

1½ teaspoons salt

1 tablespoon melted butter

1⅛ cups slightly warm milk

1. In a large bowl, mix together the flour, baking powder, and salt. Stir in the butter and warm milk until everything comes together in a sticky dough ball.

2. Knead the dough for 2 minutes on a floured surface. It should be firm and soft. Place dough in a bowl and cover it with a damp cloth or plastic wrap for at least 30 minutes but no more than 12 hours.

3. After the dough has rested, break off twelve sections and roll them into balls. Cover and let the balls rest for another 10 minutes. This step allows the gluten to develop, so that you can roll the tortilla out to a proper thickness and shape.

4. After dough has rested for a second time, flatten each ball into a circle. Carefully roll out each circle with a rolling pin until it's thin and about 8" in diameter. Set prepared tortillas aside and cover them until ready to cook.

5. Heat a dry skillet on medium-high heat. Cook each tortilla for about 30 seconds on each side until it is slightly browned and starts to puff or bubble. Place cooked tortillas under a dishtowel until you are ready to serve.

6. Store completely cooled tortillas in an airtight container for 2–3 days.

7. To reheat, place the tortillas in a 200°F oven for 2–3 minutes, but don't leave them in the oven for longer than 5 minutes, as they will begin to dry out and lose their soft, chewy texture.

Corn Tortillas

In many places in Mexico and Central America, the staple of every meal is tortillas, and no meal is complete with them. This recipe makes a fairly traditional thin Mexican-style tortilla, but if you'd like to make a more traditional Central American-style tortilla, just leave it about ¼" thick rather than rolling it thin.

HANDS-ON: 30 minutes

INACTIVE: none

READY IN: 30 minutes

DIFFICULTY LEVEL: ★ ★ ★

YIELD: Serves 8; Makes 16 tortillas

COST PER SERVING: $

CALORIES: 118

FAT: 0 g

PROTEIN: 2 g

SODIUM: 0 mg

FIBER: 1 g

CARBOHYDRATES: 26 g

SUGAR: 0 g

2 cups masa harina
1½–2 cups very warm water

1. Place the masa harina in a large bowl.

2. Add 1½ cups of the water to the masa harina. Stir to combine and let the mixture sit for 5 minutes.

3. Knead the mixture in the bowl with the palms of your hand, as if you were kneading bread dough, until it seems to soften, about 2–3 minutes. Add a little more water or masa harina to the dough as needed. It should be neither crumbly nor sticky, but soft and mostly cohesive.

4. Divide the dough into sixteen balls and prepare two pieces of wax or parchment paper. Heat a dry griddle over medium-high heat until fully heated.

5. Working with one ball at a time, place a ball of masa harina on top of a piece of wax paper. Top it with the other piece of wax paper and squish the ball flat with the ball of your hand. Using a rolling pin, roll the dough very thin, always working from the center out and rotating the paper as needed.

6. As each tortilla is rolled, place it on the hot griddle and cook until dry and beginning to brown, about 30 seconds per side. Place cooked tortillas under a dishtowel until you are ready to serve. Store completely cooled tortillas in an airtight container for 2–3 days.

7. To reheat, place the tortillas in a 200°F oven for 2–3 minutes, but don't leave them in the oven for longer than 5 minutes, as they will begin to dry out.

Instant Oatmeal

There's nothing better than waking up to a warm, creamy bowl of oatmeal on a cold morning. Old-fashioned oats and other rolled grains will work just fine in this recipe too—you'll just need to let them sit for a couple of minutes longer when you've poured in the boiling water. If you adjust the recipe, be sure not to blend more than one-third of the oats into the flour or the final oatmeal will be goopy.

HANDS-ON: 10 minutes

INACTIVE: none

READY IN: 10 minutes

DIFFICULTY LEVEL: ★

YIELD: Serves 28; Makes 14 cups dry mix

COST PER SERVING: $

 GF   DF EF

CALORIES: 188

FAT: 5 g

PROTEIN: 4 g

SODIUM: 173 mg

FIBER: 4 g

CARBOHYDRATES: 33 g

SUGAR: 7 g

10 cups quick oats, divided

⅓ cup coconut oil, in solid form (optional)

1½ cups your choice of sugar (maple sugar, brown sugar, and coconut sugar are some of my favorites; adjust amount to taste)

3 tablespoons cinnamon

2 teaspoons sea salt

2 cups dried fruit (raisins, figs, blueberries, apricots, dehydrated apples, etc.; optional)

½ cup other add-ins (flaxseed, hemp seeds, coconut flakes, chopped nuts, etc.; optional)

1. Place 3 cups of the oats in a blender and pulse to cut into small pieces. Add the coconut oil and continue to pulse until ground into a coarse flour.

2. Toss oat flour with remaining oats, sugar, cinnamon, salt, and any add-ins.

3. Store in an airtight container for up to 1 month.

4. To serve, mix ½ cup of instant oatmeal mix with 1 cup boiling water and let sit for 1–2 minutes.

CHAPTER 4

"Out of the Box"

It seems like the more you flip over cracker boxes, soup cans, and ketchup bottles to look at their ingredient lists, the less products there are that actually offer some kind of nutritional benefit. Nowadays, grocery store shelves are filled with the same undesirable ingredients—preservatives, additives, and artificial colorings—over and over again. It may seem like you have to spend hours in the kitchen just to create healthy options, but that's just not true. The recipes in this chapter will show you that you can make convenient meals without all that extra junk—and they can even taste just like those foods you love! All of these recipes are designed to "make ahead," so that you can fill your shelves and freezer with wholesome, homemade versions of your favorite foods instead of stocking them full of cans and boxes. ❧

Stovetop Macaroni and Cheese

Macaroni and cheese is a staple in many households, but depending on what country you live in (including the U.S.), your favorite meal-in-a-box might include food dyes derived from crude oil and a vast array of natural and artificial preservatives. This homemade stovetop variety of the family favorite uses natural ingredients, dirties only one pot, and can be made relatively quickly without creating a huge mess, making it the perfect meal for just about any time.

HANDS-ON: 25 minutes	
INACTIVE: none	
READY IN: 25 minutes	
DIFFICULTY LEVEL: ★ ★	
YIELD: Serves 6; Makes 6 cups	
COST PER SERVING: $ $	

CALORIES: 565	
FAT: 26 g	
PROTEIN: 23 g	
SODIUM: 476 mg	
FIBER: 2 g	
CARBOHYDRATES: 6 g	
SUGAR: 5 g	

1 pound macaroni, rice pasta, or other tubular pasta

3 egg yolks

¾ cup (6-ounce can) evaporated milk

1 teaspoon turmeric (optional)

1 pinch smoked paprika

½ teaspoon sea salt

½ teaspoon dry mustard powder

3–4 dashes hot sauce (optional)

8 ounces Cheddar cheese (about 2 cups), shredded, more to taste

4 tablespoons (½ stick) butter

1. Bring a large pot of water to a rolling boil; then toss in a few tablespoons of salt and the pasta.

2. While the pasta is cooking, whisk the egg yolks, milk, turmeric, paprika, salt, mustard, and hot sauce in a medium bowl. Set aside. Shred the cheese and set aside.

3. When the pasta just reaches al dente, about 6–7 minutes, drain very well but do not rinse. Return the empty pot to the stove and melt the butter over low heat.

4. When the butter is melted, pour in the egg-milk mixture. Whisk constantly for about 30 seconds while the sauce cooks; then add the cheese and stir to combine.

5. Toss in the pasta and stir to coat evenly; then stir constantly for 2–3 minutes until the cheese is completely melted and the sauce is creamy. Remove from heat and serve immediately.

6. Store the macaroni and cheese in an airtight container in the refrigerator for up to 2 days.

Stovetop Stuffing

Whether you want an easy stuffing for a holiday meal that doesn't take up room in the oven or just a quick meal on any given weeknight, making this homemade, whole-food stuffing is almost as easy as opening a box—and far more delicious.

HANDS-ON: 30 minutes

INACTIVE: none

READY IN: 30 minutes

DIFFICULTY LEVEL: ★ ★

YIELD: Serves 4; Makes 8 cups

COST PER SERVING: $

CALORIES: 327

FAT: 14 g

PROTEIN: 10 g

SODIUM: 775 mg

FIBER: 3 g

CARBOHYDRATES: 42 g

SUGAR: 4 g

8 thick slices of whole grain or sourdough bread, or 6 cups of dried bread cubes

4 tablespoons unsalted butter

3 stalks celery, finely chopped

1 small onion, finely chopped

1 teaspoon sea salt

1 teaspoon sage

1 teaspoon powered thyme, or the leaves from 3 fresh thyme sprigs

1 teaspoon finely chopped rosemary leaves

1¼ cups chicken stock

1. Preheat the oven to 300°F.

2. Place the bread on a baking sheet and dry them in the oven, about 8 minutes on each side.

3. Lower the oven to 200°F. Cut the bread into ½" squares and return to the oven for another 10 minutes or until needed.

4. Meanwhile, melt the butter in a large saucepan over medium heat. Add the celery, onion, and salt and sauté until translucent, but not brown, 6–7 minutes.

5. Add spices and chicken stock, stir well, and bring to a steady simmer, then stir in bread cubes until evenly coated.

6. Remove the saucepan from the heat and cover. Let the mixture sit for 5 minutes; then fluff and serve.

7. Store the stuffing in an airtight container in the refrigerator for up to 3 days.

Cream of Mushroom Soup

If a recipe calls for "cream of mushroom soup," here is your quick, natural food answer. Feel free to substitute celery, broccoli, cauliflower, or any other vegetable according to your needs. Make sure to lightly steam firm vegetables first to soften them before including them in this recipe. Best of all, once you've finished making your homemade condensed Cream of Mushroom Soup, you'll have the same amount as a standard 15-ounce can of store-bought, condensed cream of mushroom soup, making the healthy substitution incredibly simple!

HANDS-ON: 15 minutes

INACTIVE: none

READY IN: 15 minutes

DIFFICULTY LEVEL: ★ ★

YIELD: Serves 2; Makes 2 cups condensed soup base

COST PER SERVING: $ $

GF V EF

CALORIES: 400

FAT: 21 g

PROTEIN: 13 g

SODIUM: 1,405 mg

FIBER: 1 g

CARBOHYDRATES: 27 g

SUGAR: 16 g

¼ of an onion, coarsely chopped

1 clove garlic, coarsely chopped

2 tablespoons cornstarch (use tapioca starch if you're going to freeze the soup)

2 tablespoons butter, at room temperature

1 cup evaporated milk

1 tablespoon Worcestershire sauce

1 teaspoon sea salt

¼ teaspoon black pepper

⅛ teaspoon smoked paprika (optional)

1 teaspoon dried parsley (optional)

8–10 large mushrooms, any variety, coarsely chopped

1. Place all ingredients except for the mushrooms in a blender and combine until the mixture is fairly smooth. Then add the mushrooms and pulse until well blended but still a bit chunky.

2. Pour the entire mixture into a large saucepan and bring to a very gentle simmer over medium heat, about 5 minutes. Reduce heat to medium-low and continue to cook until thickened, 6–7 minutes, whisking often.

3. Use the mixture immediately or store in the refrigerator for up to 1 week. It may also be frozen for up to 3 months, although the texture may change.

4. To reconstitute, heat the condensed soup with one cup of water and simmer until heated through.

Tomato Soup

The beauty of a homemade soup is that you can season it whatever way you like, so think of this recipe as just a base. If you prefer your soups blander or stronger, just change up the herbs and spices. Also, if you plan on making this in batches to freeze, leave out the cornstarch, as it can change texture when frozen.

HANDS-ON: 5 minutes

INACTIVE: none

READY IN: 5 minutes

DIFFICULTY LEVEL: ★

YIELD: Serves 2; Makes 2½ cups condensed soup base

COST PER SERVING: $

GF

CALORIES: 294

FAT: 1 g

PROTEIN: 6 g

SODIUM: 1,350 mg

FIBER: 7 g

CARBOHYDRATES: 72 g

SUGAR: 54 g

½ **cup tomato paste**

1½ **cups tomato sauce**

2 **tablespoons dried basil**

1 **tablespoon onion powder**

1 **teaspoon dried oregano or Italian seasoning**

1 **clove garlic, minced**

2 **tablespoons unrefined cane sugar**

2 **tablespoons cornstarch**

1 **teaspoon salt**

1.   In a large bowl, whisk all ingredients until well mixed. Store in an airtight container in the refrigerator for up to 3 days, or in the freezer for up to 6 months.

2.   To reconstitute, mix 1 cup of soup base with ½ cup of water (or to taste). Bring to a simmer over medium heat; then whisk in 2 tablespoons of heavy cream or ¼ cup of milk.

Chicken Noodle Soup

On a cool, rainy Saturday, make a triple batch of this and freeze it in portions. Then when you feel a cold coming on or just need some serious comfort food, heating a portion is no more work than opening a can and provides vastly more nutrition. If you're picky about soggy noodles, keep the dry noodles out of the recipe and just add them when you serve.

HANDS-ON: 25 minutes

INACTIVE: none

READY IN: 25 minutes

DIFFICULTY LEVEL: ★

YIELD: Serves 6; Makes 3 quarts

COST PER SERVING: $ $

GF DF EF

CALORIES: 298

FAT: 12 g

PROTEIN: 22 g

SODIUM: 485 mg

FIBER: 2 g

CARBOHYDRATES: 25 g

SUGAR: 9 g

3 tablespoons butter or olive oil

1 medium yellow onion, finely minced

4 carrots, peeled and finely diced

2 celery stalks, finely diced

1 teaspoon salt, plus more to taste

3 cups chopped or shredded chicken (cooked or raw)

2 garlic cloves, minced

1 teaspoon dried thyme

8 cups chicken stock

½ cup dry soup noodles, vermicelli, or gluten-free noodles, broken into pieces

1 cup fresh or frozen peas (optional)

2 green onions, minced (optional)

1. In a large, heavy-bottomed stockpot, melt the butter over medium heat. Add the onion, carrots, celery, and salt and toss to coat. Sauté just until the onion and celery begin to wilt, 2–3 minutes.

2. If using raw chicken, toss the pieces in now and continue to sauté until cooked through, about 5 minutes, stirring frequently.

3. Add in the garlic and the thyme and sauté, about 30 seconds.

4. Add the chicken stock and bring to a steady simmer; then cover and reduce the heat to medium-low. Cook until the vegetables are fork-tender, about 10 minutes.

5. Add the dry soup noodles, peas, and cooked chicken, if using, and simmer uncovered for an additional 5–7 minutes, until noodles are cooked but not soft and the chicken is warmed through.

6. Spoon into bowls and top with minced green onions, if desired.

7. Store the chicken noodle soup in an airtight container in the refrigerator for up to 3 days or in the freezer for up to 6 months.

THE BEST WAY TO FIGHT A COLD

For an extra nutritional, feel-good punch for fighting a serious cold, add in an additional 8 cloves of garlic (minced), a 2" section of fresh ginger (cut into matchsticks), and 1 small Thai chili (minced). Toss them in just before you add the stock, and your cold will be gone before you know it!

Dry Onion Soup Mix

The store-bought powdered dry onion soup mix that comes in a package contains anti-caking agents, preservatives, and other additives, but this homemade onion soup mix features all whole-food ingredients that taste fresh and would also be great on a pot roast or added to the French Onion Chip Dip (see recipe in Chapter 2) since it makes a quick addition and adds a ton of flavor to each dish.

HANDS-ON: 5 minute

INACTIVE: none

READY IN: 5 minutes

DIFFICULTY LEVEL: ★

YIELD: Serves 8; Makes 2 cups dry mix

COST PER SERVING: $

GF V V DF EF

CALORIES: 40

FAT: 0 g

PROTEIN: 1 g

SODIUM: 596 mg

FIBER: 2 g

CARBOHYDRATES: 9 g

SUGAR: 2 g

1½ cups dried onion flakes
¼ cup onion powder
2 tablespoons parsley flakes
2 teaspoons celery seed
2 teaspoons salt
1 teaspoon ground black pepper
1 tablespoon cornstarch or arrowroot powder

1. In a large bowl, whisk all ingredients together until combined.

2. Store in an airtight container in a cool, dry place for 6–12 months.

3. To use in recipes, use ¼ cup in place of one onion soup packet.

4. To prepare as soup, stir ¼ cup into 1 cup boiling water. Serve immediately.

Baked Beans

Baked beans are the perfect addition to any barbecue! When they're slow roasted in a Dutch oven, like they are in this recipe, they're tender, scrumptious, and bursting with flavor. They also make a delicious and healthy side for any meal since you'll never have to worry about what other additives may have made it into your beans.

HANDS-ON: 15 minutes

INACTIVE: 24 hours

READY IN: 24 hours

DIFFICULTY LEVEL: ★ ★ ★

YIELD: Serves 6; Makes 9 cups

COST PER SERVING: $ $

GF V DF EF

CALORIES: 624

FAT: 18 g

PROTEIN: 22 g

SODIUM: 573 mg

FIBER: 19 g

CARBOHYDRATES: 97 g

SUGAR: 45 g

1 pound dried navy beans (about 2 cups), picked over and rinsed

1 medium yellow onion, ends trimmed, peeled, and left whole

8 whole cloves

1 (8-ounce) slab bacon or salt pork, trimmed and cut into 2" × 2" pieces (optional)

¾ cup maple syrup

¼ cup molasses

Dash of liquid smoke (optional)

2 tablespoons Dijon-style mustard

3 cups boiling water

½ cup ketchup

2 tablespoons apple cider or malt vinegar

Kosher salt and freshly ground black pepper, to taste

1. First, soak the beans. Place the beans and 10 cups of water in a large saucepan. Add a splash of vinegar, cover, then let sit for 18 hours. Drain the beans in a colander, rinse in cold water, and set the beans aside.

2. Preheat the oven to 250°F. Stud the onion with the cloves and place it in a 6-quart Dutch oven along with the beans, bacon, maple syrup, molasses, liquid smoke (if using), mustard, and boiling water. Stir to combine. Cover pot and place in the oven. Cook, stirring occasionally, for 6–7 hours, adding the ketchup and vinegar about halfway through.

3. After 6 hours, check the beans. They are finished when the beans are tender and the liquid has reduced to a thick glaze. Cook for 1–2 more hours, if needed, then season with salt and pepper.

4. Serve immediately or store in the freezer in an airtight container for up to 3 months.

Refried Beans

This dish is perfect because it's quick, frugal, and delicious! It also doubles well, if you have an 8-quart slow cooker at home. While this recipe creates thick refried beans, you can make a soupier, more authentic version by increasing the water to 8–9 cups and then re-frying them in a few tablespoons of lard. You can also tweak the seasonings to your liking, so feel free to adjust the jalapeños, cumin, and other spices however you'd prefer.

HANDS-ON: 10 minutes

INACTIVE: 9 hours

READY IN: 9 hours

DIFFICULTY LEVEL: ★

YIELD: Serves 12; Makes 12 cups

COST PER SERVING: $

GF V V DF EF

CALORIES: 66

FAT: 1 g

PROTEIN: 3 g

SODIUM: 771 mg

FIBER: 3 g

CARBOHYDRATES: 13 g

SUGAR: 1 g

3 cups dry pinto beans or black beans

6 cups water

3 medium white or yellow onions, roughly chopped

6 cloves garlic, peeled and left whole

1 jalapeño, coarsely chopped

1 teaspoon cumin

3 teaspoons sea salt

1½ teaspoons black pepper

1. Toss everything in a slow cooker and cook on high for 8–9 hours.

2. After 7 hours, check the slow cooker to make sure the beans aren't sticking to the sides. If they are, stir in an extra cup of water until it is mixed thoroughly.

3. When the beans are completely soft, purée the mixture with an immersion blender, or in a high-speed blender or food processor.

4. Serve immediately or spoon into several airtight containers with enough for 1 meal in each one, then freeze for up to 6 months.

Fish Sticks

Fish sticks tend to be a kid-friendly meal, but are a favorite finger food for adults, too! This version is breaded instead of battered, not only because it's healthier, but also because it's easier and quicker and just like the ones in a box. While the recipe calls for cod, any firm-fleshed fish, such as halibut, tilapia, or even salmon, will do.

HANDS-ON: 15 minutes

INACTIVE: none

READY IN: 15 minutes

DIFFICULTY LEVEL: ★ ★

YIELD: Serves 3; Makes 18 fish sticks

COST PER SERVING: $ $

CALORIES: 510

FAT: 8 g

PROTEIN: 54 g

SODIUM: 1,219 mg

FIBER: 7 g

CARBOHYDRATES: 55 g

SUGAR: 3 g

1 cup whole-wheat or spelt flour

2 eggs, beaten with 1 teaspoon of water

1 cup bread crumbs

1 teaspoon salt

½ teaspoon paprika

1½ pounds cod fillets

1. Prepare your breading station by placing the flour in one bowl and the eggs in another, and whisk the bread crumbs, salt, and paprika in a third bowl. Have a parchment paper–lined baking sheet at the ready.

2. Slice the fish into ½" strips. Bread each strip by dredging it first in the flour, then dipping it in the eggs, and lastly rolling it in the bread crumbs. Shake off the excess mixture after each bowl. Place breaded strips on the baking sheet.

3. Freeze on the baking sheet until fish sticks are solid, about 3–6 hours. When frozen, transfer the fish sticks to an airtight storage container and freeze for up to 3 months.

4. To bake, place the frozen fish sticks on a baking sheet and bake in a 400°F oven for 18–22 minutes, or until fish flakes easily with a fork, turning once.

Chicken Nuggets

Chicken nuggets are a great freezer option for busy days. If you find chicken breast on sale, you can stock up and make several dozen of these at a time to make sure you always have a natural, delicious meal option handy. For an even quicker result, just pound the breasts to a uniform thickness, cut each breast into eight pieces, and follow the dredging process.

HANDS-ON: 30 minutes

INACTIVE: none

READY IN: 30 minutes

DIFFICULTY LEVEL: ★ ★ ★

YIELD: Serves 4; Makes 24 chicken nuggets

COST PER SERVING: ★ ★

CALORIES: 690

FAT: 14 g

PROTEIN: 59 g

SODIUM: 712 mg

FIBER: 10 g

CARBOHYDRATES: 83 g

SUGAR: 4 g

2 cups whole-wheat or spelt flour

4 eggs, beaten with 1 teaspoon water

2 cups bread crumbs

3 chicken breasts, or 6 chicken thighs

5–6 slices uncooked bacon (optional)

Pinch of unrefined sea salt

Pinch of freshly ground black pepper

1. Prepare your breading station by placing the flour in one bowl, the eggs in a second bowl, and the bread crumbs in a third. Have a parchment paper–lined baking sheet at the ready.

2. Cut the raw chicken breasts into chunks and coarsely chop the raw bacon, if using. Place in a food processor with the salt and pepper and process until smooth.

3. Using moistened hands, form the mixture into nuggets no more than ¾" thick. Bread each nugget by dredging it first in the flour, then dipping it in the eggs, and lastly rolling it in the bread crumbs bowl. Shake off the excess mixture after each step. Place breaded nuggets on a parchment paper–lined baking sheet.

4. Freeze on the baking sheet until nuggets are solid, about 3–6 hours; then transfer to an airtight storage container. Freeze for up to 3 months.

5. To bake, place the frozen nuggets on a baking sheet and bake in a 350°F oven for 18–22 minutes, flipping once. Test for doneness by pricking one nugget with a fork; the juices should run clear.

Hamburger Patties

This is a large recipe, but keep in mind that you'll make these patties in order to stock your freezer instead of purchasing patties at the store. Made with simple ingredients and steps, these patties will provide you with the perfect base for all your favorite flavors at the time of cooking. If there are specific tastes or ingredients you always gravitate toward when making burgers, such as barbecue sauce or crumbled blue cheese, feel free to add those in the recipe, too!

HANDS-ON: 15 minutes

INACTIVE: none

READY IN: 15 minutes

DIFFICULTY LEVEL: ★

YIELD: Serves 16; Makes 16 hamburger patties

COST PER SERVING: $ $ $

CALORIES: 200

FAT: 11 g

PROTEIN: 22 g

SODIUM: 74 mg

FIBER: 0 g

CARBOHYDRATES: 1 g

SUGAR: 0 g

4 pounds ground beef

1 medium yellow onion, very finely minced

1 tablespoon liquid smoke (optional)

Salt, to taste

Pepper, to taste

1. In a large bowl, combine the ground beef, minced onion, and liquid smoke. Mix well, but handle the meat as gently and as little as possible, as overhandling can cause the meat to shrink during cooking. Divide the mixture into sixteen portions.

2. With a light touch, pat each portion into a ½"-thick patty and press a dent into the middle of each one to prevent plumping up during cooking. Too thin is better than too thick, in this case. Generously season each patty on both sides with salt and pepper.

3. Stack the patties in an airtight storage container separated by pieces of wax paper, freezer paper, butcher paper, or parchment paper and store in the freezer for up to 3 months or in a deep freeze for up to 6 months.

4. To cook, either grill the frozen patties for 15–20 minutes, until the internal temperature is 160°F, or bake them. To bake, place the patties on a baking sheet in a 400°F oven, and bake for 2–3 minutes, then reduce the temperature to 250°F and cook for another 30–35 minutes.

Black Bean Veggie Burgers

These are great burgers for tossing in the freezer and just pulling out when you're wanting a quick supper. For omnivores, vegetarians, and vegans alike, these burgers are very flexible and a perennial favorite.

HANDS-ON: 30 minutes

INACTIVE: none

READY IN: 30 minutes

DIFFICULTY LEVEL: ★ ★ ★

YIELD: Serves 12; Makes 12 patties

COST PER SERVING: $ $ $

CALORIES: 99

FAT: 1 g

PROTEIN: 4 g

SODIUM: 222 mg

FIBER: 4 g

CARBOHYDRATES: 18 g

SUGAR: 1 g

1½ cups old-fashioned or gluten-free oats

2 cups cooked black beans, or 1 (15-ounce) can black beans, drained and rinsed

1½ cups pumpkin purée or mashed sweet potato

⅔ cup cooked quinoa or brown rice

½ red pepper, minced

½ red onion, minced

6–8 stems fresh cilantro leaves, minced

2 teaspoons cumin

1 teaspoon chili powder

1 teaspoon chipotle powder or smoked hot paprika (optional)

½ teaspoon salt

1. Place the oats in a blender or a food processor and pulse until very fine, but not ground into flour. Set aside.

2. Mix all the remaining ingredients in a food processor, electric mixer, or a large mixing bowl and process until everything is well mixed. Use a food processor if you want smoothly textured burgers and a mixer if you want a chunkier texture.

3. Add in the oats and mix again until the mixture can easily be formed into a patty. Place in the refrigerator for at least 30 minutes. This helps the patties stay together as they are cooked.

4. When the mixture is well chilled, scoop out about ½ cup, press into a 3"–4" patty, and set on a baking sheet. Shape the remaining patties in the same way until the entire mixture is used.

5. At this point, you can cook the burgers right away or freeze them for later use. To freeze, place the entire baking sheet in the freezer until burgers are solid, 2–3 hours. Place the burgers in an airtight container or freezer bag separated by wax paper and freeze for up to 6 months.

6. Prepare frozen patties by baking at 350°F for 30 minutes, turning once. You can also thaw them and then pan-fry each patty over medium heat in a lightly oiled sauté pan for 3–4 minutes per side.

7. To cook immediately, preheat a sauté pan with 1 tablespoon of palm shortening or your favorite sauté oil. Pan-fry the burgers for 3–4 minutes per side; then serve as traditional burgers or topped with salsa and guacamole.

Frozen Pie Crust

Having a frozen pie crust handy means that you can make a quick meal or decadent dessert when pressed for time. In just 10 minutes, you can create a savory shepherd's pie or a sweet, aromatic apple pie with a light, flaky crust. Be sure to use a metal pie plate or tart tin for freezing, as glass likely won't go from freezer to oven without shattering.

HANDS-ON: 15 minutes

INACTIVE: 30 minutes

READY IN: 45 minutes

DIFFICULTY LEVEL: ★ ★

YIELD: Serves 16; Makes 2 pie crusts

COST PER SERVING: $

CALORIES: 181

FAT: 12 g

PROTEIN: 2 g

SODIUM: 149 mg

FIBER: 1 g

CARBOHYDRATES: 15 g

SUGAR: 0 g

2½ cups all-purpose flour

1 teaspoon sugar

1 teaspoon salt

8 tablespoons (1 stick) butter, cut into cubes and chilled

½ cup palm or other vegetable shortening

⅓ cup plus 1 tablespoon very cold water

1 tablespoon vinegar

1. Whisk the flour, sugar, and salt together in a bowl.

2. Add in the cubes of butter and shortening and quickly work them into the flour mixture. Most of the mixture should be the consistency of coarse crumbs and hold together when squeezed in your hand, but a few pieces should be the size of peas.

3. Stir the vinegar into the cold water; then drizzle the water over the flour mixture and stir it into a ball. Add 1–2 more tablespoons cold water if needed.

4. Divide the dough into two equal balls; then press each into a rough disk and set aside. Refrigerate the disks for at least 30 minutes.

5. Working from the center at all times, roll each disk out into a ⅛"-thick circle.

6. Drape each circle over a pie pan and pat into place. Feel free to flute or decorate the edges if desired.

7. To freeze, place a large piece of wax paper over one crust, then set the other crust on top, including its pan. Place the layered crusts in a large, plastic bag with as much air removed as possible or in another airtight container. Set the crusts in the freezer and store for up to 6 months.

8. To use, do not thaw, but fill and bake according to the temperatures and times of your particular recipe, adding a few minutes to compensate for the crust's frozen state.

CHAPTER 5

Meats and Dairy

Inspired by centuries of cooks who have nourished their families with these exact same methods, this chapter will show you how to culture milk into yogurt, turn salmon into lox, make butter from cream, and so much more. While all of these recipes are simple enough to recreate at home using common kitchen ingredients, some of them, especially the dairy-based ones, are easier with a starter culture. Using one will help you obtain the best flavor and consistency, and they're easily found online. Each of these dairy recipes will also include a shortcut version for the food, so that you can still make your favorite meals without relying on a purchased starter.

Yogurt

Once you get a taste of homemade yogurt and feel the satisfaction that comes with it, you'll start wondering what else you can make at home. The method described here makes a delicious plain, Balkan-style yogurt, the kind you find at any store. This recipe uses a yogurt maker, only because there are about seventeen million ways to culture yogurt and it's merely the absolutely easiest way to do it. If you don't have a yogurt maker, just find a way to keep the milk at around 112°F for 6–8 hours, like using a food dehydrator or a warmed slow cooker.

HANDS-ON: 15 minutes

INACTIVE: 10 hours

READY IN: 10 hours

DIFFICULTY LEVEL: ★ ★ ★

YIELD: Serves 8; Makes 2 quarts

COST PER SERVING: $ $

GF V EF

CALORIES: 158

FAT: 8 g

PROTEIN: 8 g

SODIUM: 112 mg

FIBER: 0 g

CARBOHYDRATES: 12 g

SUGAR: 14 g

8 cups whole milk

½ cup plain yogurt, or 2 teaspoons powdered yogurt starter (if you use store-bought yogurt, make sure it doesn't have any gelatin or other additives and double-check the quantity of powdered yogurt starter according to your brand)

1. Prepare a large saucepan with a lip by setting an ice cube in it and letting it melt at room temperature, tilting the pan every once in a while to make sure the ice water touches and covers every part of the bottom. (The ice water will keep the milk from sticking to the bottom of the pan as it scalds, and the lip on the pan will keep your pan drip-free as you pour the milk out later.)

2. Add the milk to the saucepan.

3. Heat the milk slowly to 180°F over medium-low heat, whisking occasionally, about 30 minutes. Gently heating the milk in this manner physically changes the molecular structure of the milk proteins and evaporates off a bit of water, both of which help result in a decidedly firmer yogurt.

4. Once the milk has reached 180°F or so, cool it to approximately 115°F, either by placing it in an ice bath or just letting it sit.

5. Place the yogurt starter in a small mixing bowl; then ladle in about a cup of warm milk and whisk to combine. Pour the starter mixture into the entire pot of warmed milk and stir very briefly—it's best if there are a few lumps rather than it being perfectly smooth.

6. After the mixture is combined, pour the prepared milk into your yogurt maker, or pour into slightly warm mason jars, wrap in several towels, and place in an insulated cooler.

7. Culture the yogurt between 108–112°F for 6–8 hours. If you're using the Mason jar/cooler method, don't stress about the amount of

time. Just let them sit and move them to the refrigerator after 8 hours or overnight.

8. At the end of 6–8 hours, the yogurt should be somewhat firm and pull away from the side of the container with only a bit of whey (extra liquid). Transfer your containers to the refrigerator and chill for at least 6 hours before serving. The yogurt will continue to firm up and improve in flavor as it cools.

9. Store your yogurt in the refrigerator, where it will stay fresh for 5–7 days.

YOGURT TROUBLESHOOTING

If you've got too much whey, you likely incubated longer than necessary. If the yogurt is too thin, the temperature was too high or too low, the milk wasn't fresh, or your starter wasn't sufficient, either because you didn't use enough or because the culture was old. Yogurt culture can degrade over time due to the introduction of foreign bacteria, so using a fresh starter every few batches is recommended.

Sweet Butter

Traditionally, butter has been made by churning it in a large urn. The process takes hours and is quite laborious. In the modern kitchen, however, you can make butter in mere minutes by using an electric mixer. It'll give you the same, wholesome taste and nutrition as the traditional method.

HANDS-ON: 20 minutes

INACTIVE: none

READY IN: 20 minutes

DIFFICULTY LEVEL: ★ ★

YIELD: Serves 24; Makes 3 cups

COST PER SERVING: $

GF V EF

CALORIES: 138

FAT: 15 g

PROTEIN: 1 g

SODIUM: 113 mg

FIBER: 0 g

CARBOHYDRATES: 1 g

SUGAR: 0 g

1 quart heavy cream

1 teaspoon salt

1. Pour the cream into the bowl of an electric mixer fitted with the whisk attachment. Slowly, bring the mixer up to medium speed.

2. Continue whipping for 8–10 minutes. The mixture will first look like whipped cream and then, all of a sudden, will look and sound more watery. Drain off this "butter water" and continue whipping on low for another 2–3 minutes. You want to get as much of this water out as possible.

3. Prepare a large bowl with very cold water. Gather the butter together into a ball and place it under the cold water. Knead it a few times with your hands, which releases the "butter water" and keeps the butter fresh.

4. Your butter is now ready. If desired, feel free to knead in the salt or any other additives you'd like.

5. Store your butter in a covered container in the refrigerator for up to 2 weeks.

Sour Cream

The best way to make sour cream is with a starter, either a prepackaged starter or a dollop from a previous batch, because it provides just the right flavor and texture. However, it's difficult to find probiotic sour creams in the grocery store that aren't thickened with carrageenan, which is a known irritant in the colon, or gums, which are highly processed, and both of which interrupt the natural probiotics when reculturing a new batch. Also, sometimes you don't want to wait for a purchased starter to arrive in the mail, so this recipe is perfect for when you need a nutritious, homemade batch on the fly. Keep in mind that the buttermilk will best mimic the flavor of a store-bought sour cream.

HANDS-ON: 5 minutes

INACTIVE: 24 hours

READY IN: 24 hours

DIFFICULTY LEVEL: ★

YIELD: Serves 8; Makes 1 pint

COST PER SERVING: $

  EF
GF V

CALORIES: 213

FAT: 22 g

PROTEIN: 2 g

SODIUM: 39 mg

FIBER: 0 g

CARBOHYDRATES: 2 g

SUGAR: 1 g

1 pint heavy whipping cream

½ cup cultured buttermilk, lemon juice, or white vinegar

1. Place cream in a quart-size jar and add in your acidic medium. Stir briefly.

2. If you have used buttermilk, simply cover tightly and set aside.

3. If you have used lemon juice or vinegar, observe the mixture as you stir to check if the cream has begun to curdle. If it has not thickened or curdled at all, add another tablespoon or two; then stir again.

4. Cover tightly and set aside at room temperature for 24 hours or until the mixture becomes thick. Move to the refrigerator to finish setting, 2–3 hours.

5. Store your sour cream in an airtight container in the refrigerator for up to 1 week.

Buttermilk

HANDS-ON: 5 minutes

INACTIVE: 5 minutes

READY IN: 10 minutes

DIFFICULTY LEVEL: ★

YIELD: Serves 8; Makes 2 cups

COST PER SERVING: $

CALORIES: 38

FAT: 2 g

PROTEIN: 22 g

SODIUM: 27 mg

FIBER: 0 g

CARBOHYDRATES: 3 g

SUGAR: 3 g

Culturing buttermilk can take a day or so, but if you don't have that much time or just don't want to purchase a starter culture, this homemade version will do the trick. Quick and easy, this recipe only takes a few minutes to put together and renders baked goods light and tender.

2 cups milk
2 tablespoons lemon juice

1. Place the milk in a measuring cup or bowl; then add the lemon juice and stir to combine.

2. Let sit uncovered for 5–10 minutes at room temperature. The buttermilk is finished as soon as the mixture thickens and begins to curdle.

3. Use immediately or store the buttermilk in the refrigerator in an airtight container for up to 5 days.

Cream Cheese

HANDS-ON: 5 minutes

INACTIVE: 1–2 hours

READY IN: 2 hours

DIFFICULTY LEVEL: ★ ★

YIELD: Serves 8; Makes 1 quart

COST PER SERVING: $ $

CALORIES: 142

FAT: 9 g

PROTEIN: 6 g

SODIUM: 674 mg

FIBER: 0 g

CARBOHYDRATES: 9 g

SUGAR: 9 g

The true way to make cream cheese involves a starter culture and is very easy, but if you're wanting a schmear ready for your breakfast tomorrow morning, you make labneh. It's a Middle Eastern soft cheese that stands in as a "shortcut" version of cream cheese and tastes delicious. It makes for an extra lovely treat when you add lemon juice and dried mint to it.

6 cups plain yogurt
2 tablespoons olive oil
2 teaspoons salt

1. Mix all ingredients. Pour into a cheesecloth-lined strainer; then tie up the ends of the cheesecloth to form a bag. Hang the bag to let the cheese drip out the whey and let hang for 1–2 hours. Remove after only 1 hour if you like a softer cheese and after 2 hours if you like a firmer cheese.

2. To serve, peel the cheesecloth away from the cheese and place the cheese in an airtight container. Store in the refrigerator for up to 1 week.

Liverwurst Sandwich Spread

Liver is—perhaps surprisingly—a deeply nourishing food. It has lost favor over the last several decades, but when prepared with garlic and fresh herbs and coupled with rich, creamy butter, it comes alive. Liver is like the multivitamin of the food world, only better, obviously, since the vitamins are natural rather than synthetic and easily bio-available. Vitamin A and vitamin D, especially if the animal was pastured, are present in abundance, as well as a large amount of folate. (A small 3-ounce serving of beef liver provides more than half of a woman's daily recommended intake of folate!) All the B-vitamins show up in great prominence, as does iron and the trace minerals copper, zinc, and chromium. All in all, it's food that does a body good!

HANDS-ON: 25 minutes

INACTIVE: 20 minutes

READY IN: 45 minutes

DIFFICULTY LEVEL: ★ ★

YIELD: Serves 8; Makes 2 cups

COST PER SERVING: $ $ $

GF EF

CALORIES: 150

FAT: 9 g

PROTEIN: 12 g

SODIUM: 58 mg

FIBER: 0 g

CARBOHYDRATES: 3 g

SUGAR: 1 g

1 pound beef liver, cut into pieces

1 small red onion, chopped

2 tablespoons plus 6 ounces clarified butter, at room temperature, divided

½ cup red wine

2 cloves garlic, crushed

1 teaspoon Dijon mustard

1 sprig fresh rosemary

1 sprig fresh thyme

1 tablespoon lemon juice

Sea salt, to taste

¼ cup heavy cream

Cracked black pepper, to taste

1. Sauté the liver and onions over medium heat in 2 tablespoons of the butter until the livers are browned and the onions are tender, 10–20 minutes. Add wine, garlic, mustard, herbs, and lemon juice and cook uncovered until most of the liquid has evaporated, another 8–10 minutes.

2. Cool and blend in the food processor until smooth, along with the remaining butter. Add salt to taste.

3. If the pâté is dry and crumbly rather than smooth and creamy, add more butter 1 tablespoon at a time.

4. Once the pâté is smooth but with the motor still running, slowly pour in the cream and process until the mixture is once again smooth.

5. Place the finished liverwurst in a serving dish and grind a generous amount of cracked pepper over the top.

6. Cover with plastic wrap and store in the refrigerator for up to 1 week.

Lunch Meat

Learning old-fashioned techniques makes it possible to make lunch meat at home, but be forewarned that it takes a bit of effort and skill to make it silky smooth like the store-bought version. The secret to getting the texture just right is to keep your ingredients as cold as possible and to combine them with just the right amounts of fats and water. To make lunch meat even more economically, make roast beef sandwich slices. Cook a beef roast for dinner one evening, then shave all the leftovers into thin slices for sandwiches for the rest of the week.

HANDS-ON: 30 minutes

INACTIVE: 2 hours 15 minutes

READY IN: 3 hours

DIFFICULTY LEVEL:
★ ★ ★ ★

YIELD: Serves 24; Makes 1 loaf

COST PER SERVING: $ $

GF DF EF

CALORIES: 186

FAT: 14 g

PROTEIN: 14 g

SODIUM: 291 mg

FIBER: 0 g

CARBOHYDRATES: 0 g

SUGAR: 0 g

1 pound bacon, fat and meat peeled apart

2½ teaspoons (1 packet) gelatin

⅓ cup very cold water or chicken stock

3 pounds ground beef, chicken, or pork

½ teaspoon smoked paprika (optional)

⅛ teaspoon black pepper

1 teaspoon liquid smoke

6–8 cloves garlic, peeled and coarsely chopped

1 teaspoon sea salt

2 tablespoons chopped fresh herbs (rosemary, thyme, sage)

1. Chill the blade of your food processor while you prep your ingredients.

2. Peel the fat off the bacon and chop it coarsely. You may save the meat part of the bacon for other meals or chop it and add it to this lunch meat. Set aside.

3. Meanwhile, sprinkle the gelatin over the cold water or stock, stir to moisten, and let stand in the refrigerator until needed.

4. Place the meat in a large bowl (make sure it will fit in your refrigerator!) and add the paprika, pepper, and liquid smoke. Combine the mixture with your hands; then place in the refrigerator for 5–10 minutes.

5. When the meat is thoroughly chilled, place the garlic, salt, and herbs in a food processor and pulse until the garlic is very finely chopped. With the motor running, drop the meat mixture and bacon fat into the bowl a few pieces at a time. (Work quickly to keep your processor from overheating and work in batches if necessary.) Grind until it is a smooth paste; then pour in the gelatin mixture and process until the mixture is once again smooth.

6. Return the meat mixture to the refrigerator for at least 10 minutes.

7. Lay out a piece of cheesecloth and shape the meat paste into a 3–4" diameter log; then place at one end of the cheesecloth. Roll the cheesecloth up absolutely as tightly as possible and tie the ends with kitchen twine. Place in the refrigerator for at least 30 minutes and up to 24 hours.

8. When you're ready to cook the lunch meat, preheat the oven to 375°F and boil a pot of water. Place the wrapped meat in a baking pan and create a water bath by pouring boiling water into the pan to at least halfway submerge the meat. Bake for approximately 1 hour and 15 minutes (give or take 15 minutes, depending on the thickness of the log), until the meat registers 155°F on a meat thermometer.

9. Cool completely; then using a very sharp knife, shave it into very thin slices.

10. Store in the refrigerator in an airtight container for up to 1 week.

Lox

Made popular by Jewish delis around the United States, lox and bagels—with the proper schmear of cream cheese, of course—are a favorite of many. The yeasty, salty goodness is easy to make at home as long as you have access to fresh salmon.

HANDS-ON: 15 minutes

INACTIVE: 3 days

READY IN: 3 days

DIFFICULTY LEVEL: ★ ★

YIELD: Serves 8; Makes 4 pounds

COST PER SERVING: $ $ $

CALORIES: 146

FAT: 6 g

PROTEIN: 20 g

SODIUM: 2,800 mg

FIBER: 1 g

CARBOHYDRATES: 2 g

SUGAR: 0 g

---

1 cup coarse kosher or sea salt

½ cup fresh dill (2–3 large fronds, torn)

2–3 tablespoons black peppercorns and/or dried juniper berries

2 fillets of wild salmon (2 pounds each), skin-on

1. Mix the salt and the spices together in a bowl until evenly mixed.

2. Place a long strip of plastic wrap on a baking sheet just long enough to accommodate the salmon.

3. Place one fillet of salmon face-up on the plastic wrap. Pour half of the salt mixture over the fillet; then lay the other fillet face-down on top of the first.

4. Pour the rest of the salt mixture over the fillets and pull the plastic wrap up and over the salmon as tightly as you can. If the fillets are small enough, place the wrapped fillets in a resealable plastic bag. Otherwise, place the fish in a baking pan or on a baking sheet long enough to accommodate the entire salmon. You don't want the fish to lose any of its brine!

5. Place the salmon in the refrigerator and weight it with a plate or a brick on top of it. Cure the salmon for 3 days, turning the salmon stack over once a day.

6. To serve, brush off the salt and spices and slice thinly or dice.

7. Store the lox in an airtight container in the refrigerator for up to 1 week or in the freezer for up to 6 months.

TRADITIONAL SWEDISH GRAVLAX

Swedish gravlax is the original "lox." In the Middle Ages, fishermen would salt their salmon and bury it in the sand above the high tide line, thus earning the name "grav lax" or "buried fish." Today, the tradition for making gravlax is the same as outlined in this recipe, but adds in whole cane sugar along with the salt. The resulting cured fish is served on crackers or bread with a dill-mustard sauce.

To make gravlax, add ½ cup unrefined sugar to the salt mixture in Step 1 of this recipe.

CHAPTER 6

Condiments

Switching to homemade condiments may be one of the most satisfying ways to start eating healthy, whole foods because you're making little changes that actually impact your health in big ways. Often, we assume that we're stuck with the products we find in stores, or assume that a certain condiment is simple enough that it must be made with real ingredients, but neither is true. With more and more companies including additives in their foods, it's becoming harder and harder to find condiments that are truly all-natural and good for you. The following recipes include the must-haves you'll use time and time again, as well as a few surprising sauces you won't be able to resist! 🌿

Easy-Peasy Ketchup

Everyone loves the bottled ketchup that comes from the store, but there's no reason why you can't make it at home! This homemade recipe is as close to the real, store-bought thing as you can get, and it's so easy to make that even a young child could help out. While you can serve it immediately, the flavor is best after sitting in the refrigerator for 2–3 days.

HANDS-ON: 10 minutes

INACTIVE: 20 minutes

READY IN: 30 minutes

DIFFICULTY LEVEL: ★

YIELD: Serves 12; Makes 3 cups

COST PER SERVING: $

CALORIES: 91

FAT: 0 g

PROTEIN: 2 g

SODIUM: 654 mg

FIBER: 1 g

CARBOHYDRATES: 23 g

SUGAR: 20 g

1½ cups tomato paste

⅔ cup raw honey or evaporated cane sugar

1 teaspoon blackstrap molasses (optional)

½ cup water

1 small onion, juiced, or ½ teaspoon onion powder

1 clove garlic, finely grated

1 cup apple cider vinegar

2 teaspoons sea salt

1. Place all ingredients in a large saucepan and stir together with a whisk until smooth. Heat over medium heat and bring to a boil; then reduce to medium-low and simmer uncovered for 20 minutes, stirring occasionally.

2. Remove the pan from the heat and let cool. You may serve the ketchup immediately, but the flavor greatly improves after 2–3 days. Pour into glass jars or leftover glass ketchup bottles and store in the refrigerator for up to 2 weeks.

TIMESAVING TIP

This ketchup freezes well, lasting up to 6 months. Make an extra batch and freeze in small portions; then thaw whenever you need more.

Classic Yellow Mustard

Whether you're slathering it on hot dogs, scooping it up with freshly baked pretzels, or serving it with bratwurst, mustard is a standard condiment in most households. This homemade version is so good that you'll never know that it didn't come out of a squeeze bottle, except that it's even tastier than its store-bought counterpart. One of the best parts of this recipe is that its yellow hue comes from a liberal use of ground turmeric. Not only does turmeric add that beautiful, golden color to the mustard, it is known to have a wide range of health benefits, including slowing the progression of cancer and assisting in weight loss!

HANDS-ON: 10 minutes

INACTIVE: 20 minutes

READY IN: 30 minutes

DIFFICULTY LEVEL: ★

YIELD: Serves 6; Makes 1 cup

COST PER SERVING: $

CALORIES: 20

FAT: 1 g

PROTEIN: 1 g

SODIUM: 343 mg

FIBER: 1 g

CARBOHYDRATES: 2 g

SUGAR: 0 g

½ cup dry mustard powder

½ cup water

⅓ cup white distilled vinegar

½ teaspoon sea salt

½ teaspoon ground turmeric

½ clove garlic, finely grated

1 small pinch smoked paprika

1 teaspoon cornstarch or arrowroot powder

1. Whisk everything except the cornstarch together in a small saucepan until smooth. Place over medium heat and bring to a boil, then reduce heat to medium-low and simmer uncovered until the mustard begins to thicken, 5–10 minutes, stirring often.

2. About 1 minute before you want to remove the mustard from the heat, stir the cornstarch together with 1 teaspoon of cold water. Then, while whisking, pour the cornstarch into the simmering mustard. Let cook for 1 minute to thicken.

3. Remove from heat and let stand 1 minute to set. Pour into the serving container, such as a glass jar or a squeeze bottle, to cool.

4. Store in the refrigerator for up to 2 weeks.

Dijon Mustard

To some, Dijon is the "fancy" mustard popularized on hoity-toity television commercials in the 1980s. But while it does lend a certain elegance, there's nothing terribly mysterious about this scrumptious condiment that elevates everything from sandwiches to chicken salad to a new level of deliciousness.

HANDS-ON: 20 minutes

INACTIVE: 6–12 hours

READY IN: 6 hours

DIFFICULTY LEVEL: ★

YIELD: Serves 16; Makes 1 pint

COST PER SERVING: $ $

CALORIES: 46

FAT: 1 g

PROTEIN: 1 g

SODIUM: 474 mg

FIBER: 1 g

CARBOHYDRATES: 2 g

SUGAR: 1 g

2 cups dry white wine

1 medium yellow onion, chopped

3 garlic cloves, thinly sliced

1 cup dry mustard

1 tablespoon olive oil

2 teaspoons sea salt

1. Place the wine, onion, and garlic in a saucepan over medium-high heat. Heat to boiling and simmer uncovered for 5–6 minutes. Turn off the heat, let the mixture cool, and then strain with a fine-mesh sieve. Discard the solids.

2. Pour the wine back into the saucepan and place over low heat. Pour the dry mustard into the liquid, whisking constantly, and whisk until smooth. Add the olive oil and salt and heat very slowly until thickened, whisking constantly. Generally, this takes about 2–3 minutes.

3. Pour into a pint-size glass jar and let sit at room temperature for 6–12 hours before moving to the refrigerator. Flavor will greatly improve with age, generally about 2–3 weeks. Store in an airtight container in the refrigerator for up to 3 weeks.

HONEY DIJON MUSTARD

To make traditional Honey Dijon Mustard, add 3 tablespoons of raw honey when you stir in the olive oil and sea salt in Step 2.

Whole Grain Mustard

This mustard is rustic and satisfying, and the real, honest ingredients combine beautifully. Use it as a healthy addition to sandwiches, pretzels, or as a dip for anything during Oktoberfest.

HANDS ON: 10 minutes

INACTIVE: 12 hours

READY IN: 12 hours

DIFFICULTY LEVEL: ★

YIELD: Serves 8; Makes 1 cup

COST PER SERVING: $

CALORIES: 43

FAT: 2 g

PROTEIN: 2 g

SODIUM: 296 mg

FIBER: 1 g

CARBOHYDRATES: 5 g

SUGAR: 3 g

½ cup whole mustard seeds

⅓ cup water

2 tablespoons apple cider vinegar

1 tablespoon honey

1 teaspoon sea salt

Juice of ½ a lemon

2 cloves garlic, coarsely chopped

1. Blend everything together in a food processor or a high-speed blender, adjusting consistency with additional apple cider vinegar or water as needed.

2. Pour into a pint-sized jar, then cover tightly and allow to stand at room temperature for 6 hours before transferring to the refrigerator to thicken. Store in the refrigerator for up to 4 weeks.

Honey Mustard

The sweetness in this mustard recipe is just too good to pass up. If you need to whip some up in a pinch, you can purchase dry mustard powder at the store, but using your own mix adds a flavor unlike anything else. To make your own dry mustard powder, grind whole mustard seeds in a coffee grinder or a blender until they become a powder.

HANDS-ON: 15 minutes

INACTIVE: 3 hours

READY IN: 3 hours

DIFFICULTY LEVEL: ★ ★

YIELD: Serves 16; Makes 2 cups

COST PER SERVING: $

CALORIES: 61

FAT: 1 g

PROTEIN: 1 g

SODIUM: 136 mg

FIBER: 0 g

CARBOHYDRATES: 12 g

SUGAR: 12 g

4 egg yolks

½ cup apple cider vinegar

½ teaspoon sea salt

⅔ cup honey

⅓ cup dry mustard powder

1. Pour 2" of water into a large saucepan and bring to a boil.

2. Meanwhile, whisk all ingredients in a stainless steel bowl. Reduce to a simmer and place the bowl over the boiling water bath. Cook for 8–10 minutes, whisking often.

3. When the mustard is thick, pour into a pint-size Mason jar and cool at room temperature. Store in the refrigerator for up to 4 weeks.

Cranberry Honey Mustard

Cranberries add a slight tartness to this recipe, which pairs nicely with the sweet taste of the traditional honey mustard. The beautiful red popping out throughout the condiment is another great touch, too. This recipe is perfect for any time you want to punch up a boring lunch, or create the ultimate post-Thanksgiving sandwich.

HANDS-ON: 10 minutes

INACTIVE: 2 days

READY IN: 2 days

DIFFICULTY LEVEL: ★

YIELD: Serves 16; Makes 2 cups

COST PER SERVING: $

GF V DF EF

CALORIES: 37

FAT: 1 g

PROTEIN: 1 g

SODIUM: 75 mg

FIBER: 1 g

CARBOHYDRATES: 6 g

SUGAR: 5 g

½ cup whole mustard seeds

¾ cup apple cider vinegar

¾ cup fresh or thawed frozen cranberries

¼ cup honey, more to taste

½ teaspoon sea salt

1. In a glass jar or ceramic bowl, combine the mustard seeds and vinegar. Cover and soak for 48 hours at room temperature, adding additional vinegar as needed to maintain enough liquid to cover the seeds.

2. When the seeds are a bit soft, pour the seeds and vinegar into a food processor or blender and process until the mixture takes on a slightly creamy consistency. Add cranberries, honey, and salt and blend again until smooth and creamy, 3–4 minutes. Add additional vinegar as needed. Keep in mind that it will thicken slightly while it stands.

3. You may serve immediately, but like most homemade mustards, the flavor will improve and mellow slightly after about a week. Store in the refrigerator for up to 4 weeks.

Classic Mayonnaise

The most traditional oil for this recipe is extra-virgin olive oil, whose rich flavor some people love and some find too strong. If you don't love the vibrant flavor of olive oil, simply use a more mildly flavored oil, such as sunflower oil, which has a similar nutritional profile but has a much more neutral flavor. You can also use 1 whole egg in place of the 2 egg yolks for a more neutral flavor, but the final product won't be quite as thick.

HANDS-ON: 10 minutes

INACTIVE: none

READY IN: 10 minutes

DIFFICULTY LEVEL: ★ ★

YIELD: Serves 6; Makes 1½ cups

COST PER SERVING: $

CALORIES: 338

FAT: 38 g

PROTEIN: 1 g

SODIUM: 201 mg

FIBER: 0 g

CARBOHYDRATES: 0 g

SUGAR: 0 g

2 egg yolks

3 tablespoons white wine vinegar

½ teaspoon sea salt

½ teaspoon Dijon-style mustard (optional)

1 cup extra-virgin olive or sunflower oil

1. Combine the egg yolks, vinegar, sea salt, and mustard in a blender or food processor. Pulse a few times to mix well.

2. With the motor running, drizzle in the oil as slowly as you possibly can. Ideally, it should take 4–5 minutes to pour in the entire cup of oil.

3. Store mixture in an airtight container. The mayonnaise will keep in the refrigerator for 1–2 weeks.

VARIATIONS

Substitute part of the olive oil with different oils to try different flavors:

- Use walnut oil when you're going to use the mayo for Waldorf salad.
- Use avocado oil when the mayo will be used in a BLT.
- Add gelatin to make fluffy mayonnaise. Stir ½ teaspoon of gelatin into 1 tablespoon cold water, then warm gently over low heat until dissolved, about 2 minutes. Pour the gelatin mixture into the mayo right before you add the oil.
- Use expeller-pressed canola oil for a less full-flavored mayo that tastes like the kind from the store.
- Use a blend of ⅔ cup olive oil, ¼ cup coconut oil (melted), and 2 tablespoons sesame oil for a yummy mayo for burgers.

TIMESAVING TIP

Put the oil in a squeeze bottle to make it easy to drip the oil in without spilling or getting a tired arm.

Vegan Mayonnaise

Whether you want an eggless mayonnaise because you're vegan, are dealing with an egg allergy, or are just wanting a mayonnaise that can be more safely left out at an all-day picnic, this creamy eggless mayonnaise is your answer. If you can't find palm shortening in your area, you can use coconut oil, but it will result in a much firmer mayo and will have a slight hint of coconut, which is lovely for Waldorf salads and burgers, but may not be as desirable in a ranch dip.

HANDS-ON: 5 minutes

INACTIVE: 2 hours

READY IN: 2 hours

DIFFICULTY LEVEL: ★

YIELD: Serves 24; Makes 1½ cups

COST PER SERVING: $ $

GF

CALORIES: 81

FAT: 9 g

PROTEIN: 1 g

SODIUM: 76 mg

FIBER: 0 g

CARBOHYDRATES: 1 g

SUGAR: 0 g

½ cup palm shortening

⅓ cup raw cashew pieces

½ cup coconut milk

½ teaspoon Dijon-style mustard

1 tablespoon lemon juice or white wine vinegar

¾ teaspoon sea salt

¼ teaspoon ground paprika

¼ cup extra-virgin olive oil

1.   Place palm shortening, cashew pieces, coconut milk, mustard, lemon juice, salt, and paprika in a blender or food processor and blend until very smooth. With the motor running, drizzle in the olive oil very slowly to emulsify. If at any point the olive oil doesn't emulsify, stop drizzling, as the mixture is fully saturated and emulsified.

2.   Pour into a jar and refrigerate for at least 2 hours to fully set and become firm. Store in an airtight container in the refrigerator for up 2 weeks.

Garlic–Dill Pickle Relish

For those who prefer a dill pickle relish to a sweet one, here's one to try. Feel free to add as much garlic as you like and even a grape leaf or strongly brewed black tea to create a really crisp relish. The tannins in both grape leaves and tea leaves help keep the cucumbers firm.

HANDS-ON: 15 minutes

INACTIVE: 3 days

READY IN: 3 days

DIFFICULTY LEVEL: ★

YIELD: Serves 32; Makes 1 pint

COST PER SERVING: $

CALORIES: 6

FAT: 0 g

PROTEIN: 0 g

SODIUM: 233 mg

FIBER: 0 g

CARBOHYDRATES: 1 g

SUGAR: 1 g

4–5 pickling cucumbers

2 cloves garlic, coarsely chopped

2 large stalks fresh dill, chopped (about 2 tablespoons)

1 tablespoon sea salt

4 tablespoons sauerkraut brine or fresh whey drained from plain yogurt

1 grape leaf, or 1 tablespoon very strongly brewed black tea (optional)

1. Wash cucumbers well and mince them finely. This can be done easily in a food grinder set with the largest die or by pulsing them several times in a food processor. Chop the garlic and the dill and toss all three ingredients together with the salt and the brine

2. Place mixture in a quart-size Mason jar. Add salt and brine. If you like a firm, crisp relish, add in the grape leaf or black tea. Using a kitchen spurtle or wooden spoon, press the relish mixture down and allow liquid to cover. If there's not enough liquid to cover, add filtered water. Make sure the top of the liquid is at least 1" below the top of the jar, as the mixture will expand as it ferments.

3. Cover tightly and keep at room temperature for 2–3 days before transferring to the refrigerator. Store in the refrigerator for up to 1 month.

Sweet Pickle Relish

The secret to a crisp, sweet relish is using the freshest produce you can find and giving it ample time to sit with the salt and sugar mixture, which draw out its juices and infuse it with a salty sweetness. And even though this appears to have several steps, don't be fooled into thinking this is a complicated recipe—it's actually refreshingly simple and will stock your pantry for several months.

HANDS-ON: 30 minutes

INACTIVE: 5 hours

READY IN: 5½ hours

DIFFICULTY LEVEL: ★ ★ ★

YIELD: Serves 64; Makes 1 quart

COST PER SERVING: $

GF

CALORIES: 15

FAT: 0 g

PROTEIN: 0 g

SODIUM: 443 mg

FIBER: 0 g

CARBOHYDRATES: 4 g

SUGAR: 3 g

1¼ pounds fresh pickling cucumbers, scrubbed

1 yellow or white onion

¼ cup coarse kosher salt (do not use regular salt, as the additives will change the color of the relish)

5–8 cups ice cubes or ice chips

⅔ cup white distilled vinegar

½ cup apple cider vinegar

1 cup evaporated cane juice

2 teaspoons mustard seeds

⅓ teaspoon celery seeds

1 (1") cinnamon stick

1 pinch ground allspice

1 pinch ground cloves

¼ teaspoon turmeric

1.   Chop the cucumbers and onion in a food processor or food grinder to ¼" dice and place in a large bowl. Sprinkle in the salt and stir so that the salt is well distributed. Place a tea towel directly on the surface of the cucumber and onions; then cover the towel with ice and let sit for 2–3 hours. Discard the ice and rinse the cucumber and onion mixture thoroughly in a colander or sieve.

2.   In a large saucepan, bring the vinegar, sugar, and spices to a boil. Reduce heat and simmer uncovered for 5–10 minutes, until the mixture has reduced slightly; then stir in the cucumber-onion mixture. Stir well; then spoon into jars and let cool. The relish can be served immediately but achieves the best flavor after 2–3 days. Store in the refrigerator for 1–2 months.

British-Style Steak Sauce

Chefs in Britain have perfected a thick, tangy, deeply flavorful sauce that accompanies seared meat beautifully. This is one of those recipes that seems like it should be difficult, but it takes mere minutes to make with very little effort.

HANDS-ON: 10 minutes

INACTIVE: 10 minutes

READY IN: 20 minutes

DIFFICULTY LEVEL: ★

YIELD: Serves 8; Makes 2 cups

COST PER SERVING: $ $

CALORIES: 70

FAT: 0 g

PROTEIN: 1 g

SODIUM: 174 mg

FIBER: 2 g

CARBOHYDRATES: 17 g

SUGAR: 13 g

⅔ cup chopped dates or raisins

1 cup boiling water

1 cup malt vinegar

⅓ cup tomato paste

¼ cup Worcestershire sauce

2 teaspoons tamarind paste (optional)

2 tablespoons onion juice, or 1 teaspoon onion powder

3 teaspoons blackstrap molasses

2 cloves garlic, finely minced

1. Place the dates or raisins in a small bowl and pour the boiling water over them. Soak for 5–10 minutes. Do not drain.

2. Place all ingredients, including the soaking water, in a blender and blend until smooth. Season with salt and pepper and adjust seasonings to taste.

3. Flavor is best after 1–2 days, but it may be served immediately if desired. Store the sauce in an airtight container in the refrigerator for up to 3 weeks.

KICK UP THE FLAVOR!

For deeper flavor, place the mixture in a wide, heavy-bottomed saucepan and let it simmer uncovered over medium-low heat 10 minutes. Then remove from heat and let it cool completely before serving or storing.

Chili Sauce

Sweet and spicy, chili sauce is finding its way onto more plates than ever. It imbues any meat with a surprisingly delightful flavor and adds the right amount of kick to any meal with its unique blend of ingredients. Use it as you would ketchup—on a burger, with meatloaf, or with a meat pie, such as tourtière.

HANDS-ON: 30 minutes

INACTIVE: 1½ hours

READY IN: 2 hours

DIFFICULTY LEVEL: ★ ★ ★

YIELD: Serves 16; Makes 2 pints

COST PER SERVING: $ $

GF V DF EF

CALORIES: 62

FAT: 0 g

PROTEIN: 1 g

SODIUM: 302 mg

FIBER: 2 g

CARBOHYDRATES: 15 g

SUGAR: 12 g

2 red or green bell peppers, finely diced

2 medium yellow onions, finely diced

3½ pounds tomatoes, peeled, seeded, and chopped

¾ cup apple cider vinegar

½ cup honey or unrefined cane sugar

1 (1") nub of fresh ginger, peeled and finely grated

2 teaspoons sea salt

¾ teaspoon ground allspice

¼ teaspoon ground cloves

¾ teaspoon ground cinnamon

½ teaspoon ground nutmeg

½ teaspoon celery seeds

½ teaspoon whole fennel or caraway seeds (optional)

Place all ingredients in a large saucepan or stockpot and bring to a boil over medium-high heat. Reduce heat to medium-low; then simmer uncovered, stirring often, until thick, 1–1½ hours. Adjust seasonings; then cool and refrigerate for up to 1 month.

Bold and Smoky Barbecue Sauce

In this homemade version of barbecue sauce, juicing the onion is an essential part of getting a smooth, glossy texture. You can either run the onion through a juicing machine or purée it in the blender with a bit of water and squeeze the mixture through a piece of cheesecloth until you have ½ cup of onion juice.

HANDS-ON: 15 minutes

INACTIVE: 45 minutes

READY IN: 1 hour

DIFFICULTY LEVEL: ★ ★

YIELD: Serves 6; Makes 1½ cups

COST PER SERVING: $ $

GF DF EF

CALORIES: 80

FAT: 5 g

PROTEIN: 0 g

SODIUM: 132 mg

FIBER: 0 g

CARBOHYDRATES: 9 g

SUGAR: 8 g

1 cup ketchup

1 onion, juiced (about ½ cup onion juice)

2 tablespoons apple cider vinegar

2 tablespoons Worcestershire sauce

2 tablespoons Dijon mustard

¼ cup blackstrap molasses

¼ teaspoon hot sauce (or more, to taste)

1½ teaspoons pure liquid smoke

2 tablespoons olive oil or clarified butter

2 cloves garlic, minced

¼ teaspoon black pepper

1 teaspoon chili powder

¼ teaspoon cayenne pepper

1. Whisk ketchup, onion juice, and other wet ingredients in a medium bowl, omitting oil. Set aside.

2. Heat oil in a large saucepan over medium heat. Add in garlic and spices and cook until fragrant, about 30 seconds.

3. Whisk in wet ingredient mixture and bring to a boil; then reduce heat to medium-low and simmer gently uncovered until the mixture thickens, about 20–30 minutes. Cool to room temperature before serving.

4. Store in the refrigerator in an airtight container for up to 2 weeks.

Sweet and Tangy Barbecue Sauce

If you prefer your barbecue sauce to have more sweetness than boldness, this recipe is for you. It has just the right balance of sweet and tart, and even though it uses ketchup, you can still be assured that you have full control over its ingredients, since the ketchup listed earlier in this chapter works beautifully in this recipe.

HANDS-ON: 5 minutes

INACTIVE: 1 hour

READY IN: 1 hour

DIFFICULTY LEVEL: ★

YIELD: Serves 8; Makes 2 cups

COST PER SERVING: $ $

GF DF EF

CALORIES: 70

FAT: 0 g

PROTEIN: 1 g

SODIUM: 519 mg

FIBER: 0 g

CARBOHYDRATES: 17 g

SUGAR: 15 g

1½ cups ketchup

½ cup apple cider vinegar

¾ cup water

3 tablespoons maple syrup

2 tablespoons Worcestershire sauce

¼ teaspoon ground black pepper (or more, to taste)

½ teaspoon sea salt

⅛ teaspoon cayenne pepper

Dash of hot sauce (optional)

1. Stir all ingredients together in a large saucepan; then bring to a boil over medium-high heat. Reduce heat to medium-low and simmer uncovered until thickened, about 25–30 minutes. Cool to room temperature before serving.

2. Store in the refrigerator in an airtight container for up to 2 weeks.

Guacamole

HANDS-ON: 5 minutes

INACTIVE: none

READY IN: 5 minutes

DIFFICULTY LEVEL: ★

YIELD: Serves 3; Makes 1½ cups

COST PER SERVING: $ $

GF

CALORIES: 220

FAT: 20 g

PROTEIN: 3 g

SODIUM: 403 mg

FIBER: 9 g

CARBOHYDRATES: 13 g

SUGAR: 1 g

The smooth texture and fresh taste of homemade guacamole pairs well with almost anything. From Mexican fare to sandwiches, this condiment adds the right amount of zestfulness to all your favorite foods. And in particular, avocado is loaded with healthy fats, so this guacamole will give you energy and keep you going!

2 avocados
2 cloves garlic, finely grated
½ teaspoon sea salt
Juice of ½ a small lime

1. Peel the avocado and scoop it into a bowl, being sure to discard the pit. Mash the avocado with a fork until coarse.

2. Add the garlic, sea salt, and lime juice, and continue to mash until the mixture is creamy but still somewhat chunky.

3. Serve immediately, or press a layer of plastic wrap directly into the surface of the guacemole to create a complete airlock, then store in the refrigerator for up to 24 hours.

Cocktail Sauce

HANDS-ON: 5 minutes

INACTIVE: none

READY IN: 5 minutes

DIFFICULTY LEVEL: ★

YIELD: Serves 5; Makes 1¼ cups

COST PER SERVING: $ $

GF

CALORIES: 55

FAT: 0 g

PROTEIN: 1 g

SODIUM: 622 mg

FIBER: 1 g

CARBOHYDRATES: 13 g

SUGAR: 11 g

A popular party dip, cocktail sauce can easily be made at home using all-natural ingredients. You won't have to feel so guilty about indulging in this condiment since it pairs nicely with fresh seafood, which is always good for the body. Try adding a bit of hot sauce or grating a bit of red pepper into this recipe for a delicious spin on the classic flavors of this tasty sauce.

¾ cup ketchup
¼ cup chili sauce
¼ cup finely grated horseradish
1 tablespoon fresh lemon or lime juice

1. Stir all ingredients together and serve at room temperature.

2. Store in the refrigerator in an airtight container for up to 2 weeks.

Tartar Sauce

HANDS ON: 5 minutes

INACTIVE: none

READY IN: 5 minutes

DIFFICULTY LEVEL: ★

YIELD: Serves 5; Makes 1¼ cups

COST PER SERVING: $ $

CALORIES: 322

FAT: 35 g

PROTEIN: 1 g

SODIUM: 338 mg

FIBER: 0 g

CARBOHYDRATES: 3 g

SUGAR: 0 g

Tartar sauce is the perfect combination of mayonnaise, crisp vegetables, and lemon juice. Use this recipe as a base and adjust it to your liking to create a tartar sauce that suits your tastes. Serve it as a dipping sauce for fresh seafood and vegetables.

1 cup mayonnaise
Juice of ½ a large lemon (or more, to taste)
1 tablespoon sweet pickle relish
1 tablespoon pickled capers
1 teaspoon fresh horseradish (or more, to taste)

1. Combine all ingredients in a medium bowl or a pint-size jar. Stir well, taste, and adjust to taste. If salt is needed or the sauce is too thick, add a bit of brine from the capers.

2. Store in the refrigerator in an airtight container for up to 3 days.

Mint Sauce

HANDS-ON: 5 minutes

INACTIVE: none

READY IN: 5 minutes

DIFFICULTY LEVEL: ★

YIELD: Serves 6; Makes ¾ cup

COST PER SERVING: $

CALORIES: 12

FAT: 0 g

PROTEIN: 0 g

SODIUM: 199 mg

FIBER: 0 g

CARBOHYDRATES: 2 g

SUGAR: 2 g

Once you've had this perky mint sauce with lamb, you'll understand why the British have made it a traditional part of any meal that uses lamb. You can also stir it into yogurt to make a quick Indian raita.

8–10 stems of fresh mint, leaves stripped off
Pinch of sea salt
1 tablespoon unrefined cane sugar
¼ cup boiling water
¼ cup white wine vinegar or malt vinegar

1. Finely mince the mint leaves and gently rub them with the sea salt and the sugar to fix the color and begin to draw out the mint juices, which will intensify the mint flavor.

2. Place the mint mixture in a small heatproof bowl and pour the boiling water over it. Stir to dissolve the sugar, let sit until completely cool, and then stir in the vinegar.

3. Taste and adjust seasonings; then refrigerate for 1–2 months.

Tzatziki

This traditional Greek condiment is a delicious dipping sauce for pita bread, as well as grilled meats and vegetables. The cultured yogurt and sour cream each provide the benefits of lacto-fermentation, including probiotics that strengthen the immune system, while the cucumber provides deep refreshment, especially in the hot summer months.

HANDS-ON: 10 minutes

INACTIVE: none

READY IN: 10 minutes

DIFFICULTY LEVEL: ★

YIELD: Serves 8; Makes 2 cups

COST PER SERVING: $ $

GF

CALORIES: 387

FAT: 2 g

PROTEIN: 1 g

SODIUM: 168 mg

FIBER: 0 g

CARBOHYDRATES: 3 g

SUGAR: 2 g

1 cup very thick yogurt

¼ cup sour cream

½ cucumber, grated

2 cloves garlic, minced

Zest of 1 lemon

Generous pinch of sea salt

2 tablespoons extra-virgin olive oil (optional)

1. Combine all ingredients in a small bowl and stir together. Serve immediately or let sit for at least 30 minutes before serving to meld the flavors.

2. Serve as an accompaniment to pita bread, grilled meats, or just as a general dipping sauce. Store in the refrigerator in an airtight container for up to 3 days.

Sweet-and-Sour Sauce

Sweet-and-Sour Sauce is another must-have in your pantry, as it pairs wonderfully with your favorite Chinese egg rolls and dim sum. Best of all, it's usually ready as soon as you finish putting dinner together.

HANDS-ON: 20 minutes

INACTIVE: 10 minutes

READY IN: 30 minutes

DIFFICULTY LEVEL: ★ ★

YIELD: Serves 4; Makes 1 cup

COST PER SERVING: $ $

GF V V DF EF

CALORIES: 83

FAT: 0 g

PROTEIN: 0 g

SODIUM: 119 mg

FIBER: 0 g

CARBOHYDRATES: 20 g

SUGAR: 17 g

½ cup pineapple juice

½ cup rice vinegar

¼ cup whole cane sugar, or 3 tablespoons honey plus ¼ teaspoon molasses

1 tablespoon ketchup

1 teaspoon soy sauce

½ a red bell pepper, finely minced

2 teaspoons cornstarch or arrowroot powder

1½ tablespoons cool water

1. Pour the pineapple juice into a small saucepan and bring to a simmer, uncovered, over medium heat. Reduce to ¼ cup, 5–10 minutes.

2. Meanwhile, mix the vinegar, cane sugar, ketchup, and soy sauce together. Add to the pineapple reduction and return to a simmer. Toss in the minced red pepper.

3. Mix the cornstarch and water to form a slurry; then pour into the sauce and stir to thicken. Remove from the heat to allow to cool.

4. Store in the refrigerator for 2–3 weeks.

Plum Sauce

Plum Sauce is another great condiment for homemade versions of your favorite Chinese takeout foods. This version is delicious right after it's made but can also be frozen for up to 6 months, so make a large batch and have plum sauce ready to go the next time you get a hankering for dim sum.

HANDS-ON: 30 minutes

INACTIVE: 30 minutes

READY IN: 1 hour

DIFFICULTY LEVEL: ★

YIELD: Serves 8; Makes 2 cups

COST PER SERVING: $ $

GF V DF EF

CALORIES: 100

FAT: 0 g

PROTEIN: 1 g

SODIUM: 2 mg

FIBER: 2 g

CARBOHYDRATES: 25 g

SUGAR: 22 g

1½ pounds plums (7–8 plums), pitted and coarsely chopped

½ cup pumpkin purée

¼–½ cup honey or whole cane sugar, depending on the ripeness of the plums

1 teaspoon onion juice, or ¼ teaspoon onion powder

½ teaspoon molasses

2 tablespoons grated ginger

¼ teaspoon crushed red pepper flakes

2 cloves garlic, finely minced

1 teaspoon ume plum vinegar or rice wine vinegar

1. Simmer the plums in a large saucepan on medium-low heat uncovered until they are very soft and beginning to fall apart, 20–30 minutes. Push the plums through a fine-mesh sieve or a food mill to remove the skins—you should end up with about 1½ cups plum purée.

2. Return the plum purée to a clean saucepan and add in the pumpkin purée, honey, onion, molasses, ginger, red pepper flakes, garlic, and vinegar. Whisk to combine.

3. Bring to a boil, uncovered, over medium-high heat; then reduce heat to medium-low and simmer gently for 5–10 minutes until slightly thickened. For a thicker sauce, simmer for an additional 5–10 minutes.

4. To serve, cool completely. Store in the refrigerator in an airtight container for up to 1 week.

Asian Dipping Sauce

This Japanese sauce is a lovely table sauce for potstickers, roasted vegetables, and grilled chicken—and it's delicious with other westernized versions of Asian cuisines as well. Since this sauce is not cooked, it's definitely preferable to use raw honey and unpasteurized, naturally fermented soy sauce (nama shoyu), as the probiotic goodness and the live enzymes are vital for our health. À votre santé! (Or rather, I should say, itadakimasu!)

HANDS-ON: 10 minutes

INACTIVE: 15–30 minutes

READY IN: 30 minutes

DIFFICULTY LEVEL: ★

YIELD: Serves 6; Makes 1½ cups

COST PER SERVING: $ $

GF V DF EF

CALORIES: 97

FAT: 5 g

PROTEIN: 3 g

SODIUM: 2,397 mg

FIBER: 1 g

CARBOHYDRATES: 10 g

SUGAR: 7 g

1 cup soy sauce

1 (2") piece of ginger, peeled and finely grated

4 cloves garlic, finely grated

2 tablespoons toasted sesame oil

2 tablespoons rice vinegar

2 tablespoons raw honey or whole cane sugar

1 tablespoon toasted sesame seeds

Pinch of dried dulse flakes (optional)

1. Stir together the soy sauce, ginger, garlic, sesame oil, rice vinegar, and honey and let stand 15–30 minutes before serving. Sprinkle in the sesame seeds and dulse flakes, if using, just before serving.

2. For best flavor, serve immediately, but if you must store the sauce, place it in an airtight container and store in the refrigerator for up to 24 hours.

Teriyaki Sauce

Many of the ingredients for this recipe are very commonly found, but only in mass-produced versions that are laden with refined sugar and preservatives. Authentic ingredients, on the other hand, are very simply crafted and use traditional brewing methods. They may take a bit of research to find, but you'll be able to recognize them by their list of ingredients. Authentic mirin, for example, uses only sweet rice, water, and rice koji culture, with perhaps a bit of sea salt. True sake is also cultured with rice koji and is akin to a good wine. Look for it in any well-stocked liquor store. As for soy sauce, try to find nama shoyu, which is packed with digestive enzymes. This sauce is heated in order to thicken it, but if you're using it as a dipping sauce, feel free to leave it raw.

HANDS-ON: 10 minutes

INACTIVE: 30 minutes

READY IN: 40 minutes

DIFFICULTY LEVEL: ★

YIELD: Serves 8; Makes 2 cups

COST PER SERVING: $ $ $

GF V DF EF

CALORIES: 133

FAT: 0 g

PROTEIN: 1 g

SODIUM: 902 mg

FIBER: 0 g

CARBOHYDRATES: 21 g

SUGAR: 17 g

1 cup mirin, or 1 cup dry sherry

½ cup sake or dry white wine

½ cup soy sauce

½ cup pineapple juice

6 tablespoons raw honey

1 (3–4") piece of gingerroot, sliced into coins

1. Whisk together the mirin, sake, soy sauce, pineapple juice, and honey in a medium saucepan. Add ginger coins.

2. Place over medium-high heat and bring to a boil; then reduce heat to medium-low and simmer uncovered for 15–20 minutes, until the mixture has thickened slightly.

3. Remove from the heat and cool completely. Serve immediately or place in an airtight container and store in the refrigerator for up to 1 week.

Peanut Sauce

Peanut Sauce will add an earthy, slightly spicy flavor to any meal you create. For best results, pair it with pad thai or use it as a dipping sauce for satays.

HANDS-ON: 10 minutes

INACTIVE: none

READY IN: 10 minutes

DIFFICULTY LEVEL: ★

YIELD: Serves 7; Makes 1¾ cups

COST PER SERVING: $ $ $

GF V DF EF

CALORIES: 167

FAT: 14 g

PROTEIN: 6 g

SODIUM: 27 mg

FIBER: 2 g

CARBOHYDRATES: 8 g

SUGAR: 5 g

1 cup dry roasted, unsalted peanuts

2 cloves garlic, minced

½ teaspoon raw soy sauce (nama shoyu)

2 teaspoons toasted sesame oil

2 tablespoons Sucanat, coconut sugar, or evaporated cane juice

2 tablespoons fish sauce or soy sauce

½ teaspoon tamarind paste, or 2 teaspoons lime juice plus ½ teaspoon blackstrap molasses

½ teaspoon cayenne pepper, or 1 teaspoon Thai chili sauce (can use more or less, to taste)

⅓ cup coconut milk

Additional water or coconut milk, for blending

1. Place all ingredients in a blender or food processor and process until smooth. If the mixture is too thick, add a bit more coconut milk or water to get the mixture to move.

2. Adjust the flavor by adding more soy sauce (to deepen flavor), sugar (to sweeten), fish sauce (to make it saltier), lime juice (if it's too salty), or cayenne (if it's not spicy enough).

3. Serve immediately or refrigerate for up to 2 weeks. Serve warm or at room temperature.

Sriracha

Sriracha is a Thai hot sauce made of chili peppers and garlic. It's made through the traditional method of lacto-fermentation, so while it takes a few days to make and the flavor continues to improve over the course of a few weeks, it's well worth the wait. Be sure to try it on eggs, pizza, or stir-fries, as sriracha elevates them all to new levels.

HANDS-ON: 30 minutes

INACTIVE: 5–8 days

READY IN: 8 days

DIFFICULTY LEVEL: ★ ★

YIELD: Serves 24; Makes 1½ cups

COST PER SERVING: $

CALORIES: 24

FAT: 0 g

PROTEIN: 1 g

SODIUM: 444 mg

FIBER: 0 g

CARBOHYDRATES: 6 g

SUGAR: 4 g

1½ pounds red hot chili peppers, preferably serranos or Fresnos, coarsely chopped and with stems snipped but green tops left intact

1 dried chipotle pepper, coarsely chopped

10 cloves garlic, peeled and left whole

¼ cup unrefined cane sugar + 1 tablespoon

1½ tablespoons sea salt

½ cup white distilled vinegar

1. Place peppers, garlic, ¼ cup sugar, and salt in a food processor. Pulse until chilies are very finely chopped, scraping the sides of the bowl as necessary. Transfer mixture to a clean jar, cover with a paper towel secured by a rubber band, and let sit at room temperature for 5–8 days

2. Check the jar each day for fermentation, denoted by the little bubbles that form throughout the mixture. Let ferment until chilies are no longer rising in volume, usually about 7–8 days.

3. Transfer chilies to a blender, add in white vinegar, and purée until completely smooth, 1–3 minutes. Transfer to a mesh strainer set on top of a medium saucepan. Strain mixture into saucepan, using a rubber spatula to push through as much pulp as possible; only seeds and larger pieces of chilies should remain in strainer.

4. Stir in the remaining tablespoon of sugar, then bring mixture to a boil, reduce heat to medium-low, and simmer uncovered until sauce thickens and clings to the back of a spoon, 5–10 minutes. Let cool, then transfer to an airtight container and store in refrigerator for up to 6 months.

Classic Hot Sauce

This hot sauce will be only as spicy as the peppers you use, so if you like a screamingly hot sauce, use Scotch bonnets or habaneros and leave the seeds in. If you like something much demurer, choose jalapeños and deseed them. This recipe uses a slightly different technique to make hot sauce than what you might find in other cookbooks. By leaving the chilies whole as they ferment, you'll find that the flavors deepen and the final result is smoother in texture. It also leaves a chili paste behind, which is delicious when added to soups, scrambled eggs, and other dishes needing a bit of a kick.

HANDS-ON: 15 minutes

INACTIVE: 5–7 days

READY IN: 7 days

DIFFICULTY LEVEL: ★

YIELD: Serves 32; Makes 1 pint

COST PER SERVING: $

CALORIES: 4

FAT: 0 g

PROTEIN: 0 g

SODIUM: 222 mg

FIBER: 0 g

CARBOHYDRATES: 1 g

SUGAR: 0 g

½ **pound fresh chili peppers**

1 **tablespoon unrefined sea salt**

1 **cup filtered water, plus more as needed**

3–4 **cloves garlic, minced**

¼ **cup white wine vinegar (or more, to taste)**

1. Remove the stems from the chilies but don't remove the cap. Chop them very coarsely and place them in a quart-size Mason jar. (If you're using small red Thai chilies, there is no need to chop them at all.)

2. Stir the salt into the water; then pour it over the chilies. If the water doesn't cover the chilies completely, add more water until they're submerged.

3. Cover loosely; then set aside at room temperature and allow to ferment for 5–7 days.

4. After 5–7 days, strain the brine off the chilies and reserve it for other fermentation projects.

5. Place the fermented chilies in a food processor or blender along with the garlic, the vinegar, and a tablespoon or two of the reserved brine. Blend until smooth.

6. Pour the mixture into a fine-mesh sieve set over a bowl. Let all the liquid drain out, pressing on the solids to extract as much liquid as possible.

7. Bottle the liquid hot sauce in an airtight container and store either in the refrigerator or at room temperature for up to 6 months. Spoon the remaining chili paste into an airtight container and store in the refrigerator for up to 6 months as well.

Harissa

Authentic harissa is a North African hot chili paste and is gorgeously spicy and intensely hot, but this recipe calls for a tamer version of the traditional paste. By substituting some of the hot peppers with sweet red peppers, the original flavor is mimicked, and the heat is provided by smoked paprika, a dried chili, and chili powder. Use harissa as a fiery condiment for pretty much anything: a sandwich spread, a grilling spice rub, a tableside bread spread, on fajitas—you name it.

HANDS-ON: 30 minutes

INACTIVE: none

READY IN: 30 minutes

DIFFICULTY LEVEL: ★ ★ ★

YIELD: Serves 32; Makes 2 cups

COST PER SERVING: $

GF

CALORIES: 40

FAT: 4 g

PROTEIN: 0 g

SODIUM: 77 mg

FIBER: 1 g

CARBOHYDRATES: 2 g

SUGAR: 1 g

---

4 large red bell peppers

2 dried red chilies, such as ancho, or 2 tablespoons dried chili flakes (or more, to taste)

2 teaspoons coriander seeds

1 tablespoon caraway seeds

½ teaspoon cumin seeds

¼ teaspoon dried mint leaves

4 large garlic cloves, unpeeled

1 teaspoon smoked hot paprika

1 tablespoon chili powder

Juice of ½ a lemon (or more, to taste)

1 teaspoon sea salt

½ cup extra-virgin olive oil

Salt and pepper, to taste

---

1.   First, roast the peppers and rub off the seeds and skins. Place in a food processor.

2.   Meanwhile, soften the dried peppers by placing in warm water for about 20 minutes. Remove the stems and seeds and place in the food processor along with the red peppers. If using dried chili flakes, just add to food processor.

3.   Toast coriander seeds, caraway seeds, and cumin seeds in a small skillet over medium heat until fragrant, approximately 1 minute. Place in a spice grinder or mortar with the mint leaves and pulverize until smooth.

4.   Meanwhile, roast the garlic. Place the unpeeled garlic cloves in a small, dry skillet and cook over medium heat until slightly blackened and soft, 4–7 minutes, depending on the size of the cloves. Set aside to cool.

5.   Place the powdered spices, paprika, chili powder, peeled garlic, lemon juice, and salt in the food processor along with the peppers and process until fairly smooth. With the motor running, drizzle in the oil very slowly until you have a smooth paste. Add salt and pepper as desired.

6.   Serve immediately or store in the refrigerator in an airtight container for up to 1 week.

Sauerkraut

This recipe, which is the classic way to preserve cabbage and which has been made for hundreds of years by peoples around the world, always turns out a delicious condiment that makes a great topping for hot dogs and other sandwiches.

HANDS-ON: 15 minutes

INACTIVE: 14 days

READY IN: 14 days

DIFFICULTY LEVEL: ★

YIELD: Serves 8; Makes 1 quart

COST PER SERVING: $

CALORIES: 28

FAT: 0 g

PROTEIN: 1 g

SODIUM: 1,788 mg

FIBER: 3 g

CARBOHYDRATES: 6 g

SUGAR: 4 g

1 medium head of cabbage (about 2 pounds), shredded
2 tablespoons sea salt

1. Place all the ingredients in a large bowl. With very clean hands, knead and massage the mixture until the vegetables begin to go limp and they release their juices.

2. Pack the mix into a sterilized Mason jar, pushing down on it as you go to release more juice. If the vegetables are not covered in brine once you reach the top, add more salt water to completely submerge them.

3. Cover tightly with a lid or a fermentation airlock (remember to burp the jar daily if using regular Mason jar lid).

4. Set aside at room temperature for 10–14 days, adding a bit of salt water each day if the top vegetables become dry. Refrigerate when the flavor is to your liking—the flavor will continue to improve for several months. The sauerkraut can stay in the fresh in the refrigerator for up to 6 months.

Kimchi

There are a few tricks to making a good, authentic kimchi. First, don't shred your vegetables like you do when making a typical sauerkraut. Part of the loveliness of kimchi is its chunky texture. Second, kimchi is supposed to be blisteringly hot: Don't skip the chilies (although you can tame them down a bit if you're not a fan of heat). And third, use Napa cabbage if at all possible. It's not only the most authentic; it has the highest levels of cancer-fighting phytonutrients.

HANDS-ON: 20 minutes

INACTIVE: 2–3 days

READY IN: 3 days

DIFFICULTY LEVEL: ★

YIELD: Serves 16; Makes 2 quarts

COST PER SERVING: $ $

GF DF EF

CALORIES: 21

FAT: 0 g

PROTEIN: 1 g

SODIUM: 1,775 mg

FIBER: 1 g

CARBOHYDRATES: 5 g

SUGAR: 2 g

1 head of Napa cabbage

¼ cup sea salt

2 cups warm water, plus more as needed

¼ cup chili-garlic paste, or 4–5 fresh red chilies, stemmed and finely minced

6–8 cloves garlic, minced

1 (2") nub of ginger, peeled and sliced into thin matchsticks

3–4 green onions, white and green parts julienned in 1" pieces

1 tablespoon fish sauce

1 cup water

1 medium pear or apple (any variety), peeled and coarsely chopped

1 small onion (any variety), coarsely chopped

1. Tear the cabbage into large, bite-size pieces and place in a large bowl. Stir the salt into the warm water to dissolve; then pour over the reserved cabbage. If the cabbage is not completely submerged, add more warm water until the cabbage is fully covered. Let sit for 3–4 hours, until the cabbage is slightly wilted; then drain and rinse.

2. Return the cabbage to the bowl and add the chili paste, garlic, ginger, green onions, and fish sauce.

3. Meanwhile, place the water, pear, and onion in a blender. Purée the mixture until smooth; then pour over the cabbage mixture. Toss everything together (be sure to wear gloves!).

4. Pack into two quart-size Mason jars, pressing down on the solids as you fill to create a brine. Add enough water to completely submerge the vegetables, if necessary, being sure to leave at least 1" of headspace in each jar. Cover tightly with lids or fermentation airlocks (remember to burp the jar daily if using regular Mason jar lid).

5. Let sit at room temperature for 2–3 days before moving to the refrigerator. The flavor will continue to develop and is best after an additional 3–4 weeks. Store in the refrigerator for up to 2 months.

Curtido

Curtido is a delicious shredded vegetable ferment that serves as an excellent accompaniment to any spicy food, especially Mexican and Central American foods. It is one of the national foods of El Salvador, where you can find it on the table of every corner pupusería to accompany the thick corn tortilla pupusas stuffed with meat, beans, and cheese. In this recipe, don't skimp on the oregano and the onions—they are the ingredients that make curtido so delicious. If you happen to have fresh loroco on hand, an herb native to Central America, you can toss a bit of that in, too.

HANDS-ON: 10 minutes

INACTIVE: 10–14 days

READY IN: 14 days

DIFFICULTY LEVEL: ★

YIELD: Serves 8; Makes 1 quart

COST PER SERVING: $

GF V V DF EF

CALORIES: 52

FAT: 0 g

PROTEIN: 2 g

SODIUM: 931 mg

FIBER: 4 g

CARBOHYDRATES: 12 g

SUGAR: 6 g

1 small head of cabbage (about 2 pounds), shredded

1 red or yellow onion, thinly sliced

4 carrots, peeled and shredded

1 chile de árbol, seeded and finely minced

1 teaspoon oregano

1 tablespoon sea salt

1. Place all the ingredients in a large bowl. With very clean hands, knead and massage the mixture until the vegetables begin to go limp and they release their juices.

2. Pack the mix into a sterilized Mason jar, pushing down on it as you go to release more juice. If the vegetables are not covered in brine once you reach the top, add more salt water to completely submerge them.

3. Cover with a clean tea towel. Set aside at room temperature for 10–14 days, adding a bit of salt water each day if the top vegetables become dry. Refrigerate when the flavor is to your liking—the flavor will continue to improve for several months. The curtido can stay fresh in the refrigerator for up to 6 months.

CHAPTER 7

Pantry Staples

Did you know you can make your own powdered sugar by placing any sugar you like in a blender and blitzing it until it's pulverized? Or that making pumpkin purée for your holiday pumpkin pie is as easy as baking a pumpkin and then smoothing it out with an immersion blender? This chapter shows the myriad ways you can easily make your favorite pantry staples, from peanut butter and vanilla extract to vinegar and Worcestershire sauce. You'll be surprised how many pantry staples you can make at home with wholesome ingredients instead of buying the less healthy versions at the store. 🌾

Pumpkin Purée

One of the best parts of roasting a pumpkin is roasting the seeds, which are a delicious, nutritious snack. As you hollow out the pumpkin, set the seeds aside, and while the pumpkin is roasting, tackle the somewhat laborious task of washing them. Then boil them for 10 minutes, pat them dry, and toss them in olive oil and salt. Roast them for 15–20 minutes at 325°F, stirring every 5 minutes or so, just until they're beginning to brown. They'll be crisp and crunchy and become a new favorite autumnal treat.

HANDS-ON: 15 minutes

INACTIVE: 1 hour

READY IN: 1½ hours

DIFFICULTY LEVEL: ★

YIELD: Serves 3; Makes 3 cups

COST PER SERVING: $ $

CALORIES: 116

FAT: 0 g

PROTEIN: 4 g

SODIUM: 4 mg

FIBER: 2 g

CARBOHYDRATES: 29 g

SUGAR: 6 g

1 pumpkin, approximately 3 pounds

1. Preheat the oven to 350°F.

2. Rinse the pumpkin under warm water, removing any dirt or debris; then cut the pumpkin in half.

3. Scoop out the seeds and set aside.

4. Lay the pumpkin face-down in a large baking dish and cover the bottom of the dish with ¼" of water.

5. Bake for 45–60 minutes or until tender.

6. Remove from the oven and scoop out the squash, discarding the skin.

7. The roasted pumpkin is now ready to use, but if you'd like a smooth texture, purée it with an immersion blender or a food processor. For an ultra-smooth texture, pass the mixture through a fine-mesh sieve.

8. Store in an airtight container in the refrigerator for up to 5 days, or in the freezer for up to 6 months.

Powdered Sugar

Powdered sugar is an essential ingredient in most baking recipes, and this one is not only easy to create; it's also much better for your body than the store-bought kind. And why arrowroot, you might ask? It's merely here as an anticaking agent so that as your homemade powdered sugar sits over time, it won't solidify into lumps. Also, depending on the sugar you use, your homemade powdered sugar may not end up being completely white. The result may be slightly darker than store-bought, but it will taste just as great.

HANDS-ON: 10 minutes

INACTIVE: none

READY IN: 10 minutes

DIFFICULTY LEVEL: ★

YIELD: Serves 10; Makes 1¼ cups

COST PER SERVING: $

CALORIES: 81

FAT: 0 g

PROTEIN: 0 g

SODIUM: 0 mg

FIBER: 0 g

CARBOHYDRATES: 21 g

SUGAR: 20 g

1 cup unrefined cane sugar, coconut sugar, or other crystalline sugar
1 tablespoon arrowroot powder

1. Place the sugar and the arrowroot powder in a blender. Bring the blender up to full speed and blend for 1–2 minutes. Let the dust settle and check for fineness. If it's not fully powdered, process for another 30–60 seconds. Blending times will vary according to the type of sugar you use.

2. Store in an airtight container for 6–9 months.

Gelatin Squares

Jello-O is one food item that most people assume has to come from a box, but the popular snack's famous jiggle can be easily and healthily replicated simply by using fruit juice and gelatin. When properly sourced, gelatin is actually a very nutritious ingredient: It provides a tremendously high percentage of protein and minerals per gram, aids digestion, seals the gut, aids liver function, and can even help relieve ulcers and acid reflux. No wonder gelatin has been served in hospitals for decades! If possible, use gelatin sourced from humanely raised, grass-fed beef rather than feedlot pigs (see the Appendix at the back of this book if you can't find it in your area). And even though this recipe makes fairly firm squares that you can pick up with your fingers, feel free to reduce the amount of gelatin to make a softer, more spoon-able dish.

HANDS-ON: 10 minutes

INACTIVE: 2 hours

READY IN: 2 hours

DIFFICULTY LEVEL: ★

YIELD: Serves 9; Makes 9 3" squares

COST PER SERVING: $ $

CALORIES: 64

FAT: 0 g

PROTEIN: 3 g

SODIUM: 11 mg

FIBER: 0 g

CARBOHYDRATES: 13 g

SUGAR: 9 g

4 cups pure fruit juice
4½ tablespoons (5 packets) gelatin
¼ cup raw honey (optional)

1. Place a 9" × 9" square baking pan at the ready.

2. Pour juice into a medium, heavy-bottomed saucepan. Sprinkle gelatin over juice and stir to break up the clumps. Turn the heat on medium-low and bring to a very gentle simmer, 5–7 minutes. Simmer and stir until gelatin is dissolved, another 1–2 minutes. Turn off heat and add honey, if using.

3. Pour into baking dish and refrigerate until set and the middle jiggles, about 2 hours.

4. Cut into 9 squares and either serve immediately or store in the refrigerator for up to 5 days.

Bread Crumbs

Bread crumbs are a handy item to have on hand to make a crispy coating to foods that will be baked, such as chicken nuggets and fish sticks. The popular brands on the market contain preservatives and anticaking agents, but by making your own, you've got much more control over the ingredients. And if you save the ends of your loaves of bread as you use them up, you can save money too, as those ends make lovely bread crumbs!

HANDS-ON: 10 minutes

INACTIVE: 15–20 minutes

READY IN: 30 minutes

DIFFICULTY LEVEL: ★

YIELD: Serves 8; Makes 4 cups

COST PER SERVING: $

CALORIES: 92

FAT: 1 g

PROTEIN: 4 g

SODIUM: 208 mg

FIBER: 1 g

CARBOHYDRATES: 18 g

SUGAR: 1 g

8 slices of bread, any variety, torn into pieces

1. Preheat the oven to 300°F.

2. Place the bread pieces on an ungreased baking sheet and bake until dry, about 15 minutes, tossing the pieces if they seem to be browning too much.

3. Place the torn pieces in a food processor and pulse until even crumbs are formed, 3–5 minutes. Alternatively, you can place the pieces in a large zippered plastic bag and crush them with a rolling pin.

4. Use the bread crumbs immediately or store in the freezer for up to 3 months.

All-Purpose Baking Mix

HANDS-ON: 5 minutes

INACTIVE: none

READY IN: 5 minutes

DIFFICULTY LEVEL: ★

YIELD: Serves 6; Makes 6½ cups dry mix

COST PER SERVING: $ $

CALORIES: 707

FAT: 35 g

PROTEIN: 11 g

SODIUM: 1,370 mg

FIBER: 3 g

CARBOHYDRATES: 86 g

SUGAR: 4 g

Baking mix is an incredibly useful item to have on hand, as you can mix up pretty much any baked good in a flash. Pancakes, biscuits, dumplings, muffins—you name it! Use this mix measure-for-measure in any of your favorite recipes calling for store-bought baking mixes, like Bisquick.

5 cups all-purpose flour, whole-wheat flour, or spelt flour

¼ cup baking powder

2 tablespoons unrefined cane sugar

1 teaspoon sea salt

1 cup palm shortening or butter

1. Mix the dry ingredients together in a large bowl. Cut in the shortening with a fork, a pastry cutter, or your fingertips until the mixture resembles fine crumbs. Use in any recipe that calls for store-bought baking mix, like Bisquick.

2. Store in an airtight container at room temperature for up to 2 months, or in the freezer for up to 6 months.

Baking Powder

HANDS-ON: 5 minutes

INACTIVE: none

READY IN: 5 minutes

DIFFICULTY LEVEL: ★

YIELD: Serves 16; Makes 1 cup

COST PER SERVING: $

CALORIES: 19

FAT: 0 g

PROTEIN: 0 g

SODIUM: 946 mg

FIBER: 0 g

CARBOHYDRATES: 5 g

SUGAR: 0 g

Making your own baking powder may feel like you're going a bit far on the whole "make all my own pantry basics from scratch" spectrum, but if you're needing to avoid corn or wanting to avoid aluminum in your diet, making your own is the way to go. Most commercial baking powders contain cornstarch to keep everything from clumping (which may be genetically modified corn in a few cases) and about half of the store-bought brands use sodium aluminum sulfate, which is a mildly acidic leavening agent. Cream of tartar, on the other hand, is a mildly acidic powder left over from the fermentation of grapes during winemaking and contains no heavy metals.

¼ cup baking soda

½ cup cream of tartar

¼ cup arrowroot powder

Mix thoroughly, and store in an airtight container for up to 6 months.

White Wine Vinegar

Vinegar is easy and fun to make—especially if you are a wine connoisseur and have various bottles of wine around. Vinegar is essentially alcohol that has overfermented and turned into acetic acid, so it's a great way to use up leftover wine that no longer tastes that great. This recipe uses white wine, but if you are a red wine lover, feel free to substitute your favorite bottle to create a red wine vinegar. You'll find that homemade vinegar has a much different taste than store-bought—it's fuller and richer, and doesn't have as much harsh bite to it.

HANDS-ON: 15 minutes

INACTIVE: 12 weeks

READY IN: 12 weeks

DIFFICULTY LEVEL: ★ ★

YIELD: Serves 32; Makes 1 gallon

COST PER SERVING: $

CALORIES: 72

FAT: 0 g

PROTEIN: 0 g

SODIUM: 4 mg

FIBER: 0 g

CARBOHYDRATES: 2 g

SUGAR: 1 g

1 vinegar starter, or "Mother of Vinegar"
12 cups white wine, divided
5 cups water

1. Place your vinegar starter into a large (at least 1 gallon) glass or ceramic jar with a spigot at the bottom. Add 6 cups of wine and 3 cups of water.

2. Cover the top of your crock with a cheesecloth and attach it firmly with a rubber band. This keeps out insects, but lets in the oxygen that makes the process happen.

3. Add 1–2 cups of white wine once a week or so, plus ½–1 cup water until you've added all 12 cups wine.

4. Wait a total at least 12 weeks; then do a taste test. If it smells like vinegar and tastes like vinegar, it's ready! If not, let it sit another week or two. When it's ready, pour into old vinegar jars or flip-top bottles. (A funnel helps tremendously with this.)

VINEGAR STARTERS, OR MOTHERS

A "mother" is a combination of cellulose and acetic acid bacteria. It uses oxygen from the air to turn alcohol into acetic acid, and usually looks like a cloudy mass that sits at the bottom of the crock. You can get a vinegar mother from a beer and wine–making supply store or online.

Homemade Pasta

For some of the world, noodles are traditionally made with merely flour and water. In other parts, traditional pasta is made with flour and eggs. But for modern cooks who like things richly flavorful yet easy to put together, pasta is made with flour, eggs, olive oil, and salt. This gives the greatest elasticity to the dough and makes the pasta light and rich as it cooks. Make sure you give yourself time to knead the dough and let it rest properly. These steps are essential for achieving a soft, elastic dough.

HANDS-ON: 30 minutes

INACTIVE: 30 minutes

READY IN: 1 hour

DIFFICULTY LEVEL: ★ ★

YIELD: Serves 4; Makes 2 pounds cooked pasta

COST PER SERVING: $

CALORIES: 291

FAT: 5 g

PROTEIN: 11 g

SODIUM: 348 mg

FIBER: 2 g

CARBOHYDRATES: 48 g

SUGAR: 0 g

2 cups flour (all-purpose, spelt, or whole-wheat)

3 eggs

½ teaspoon sea salt

1 teaspoon olive oil

MAKE PASTA WITH A STAND MIXER

1. Place all ingredients in the bowl of a stand mixer fitted with a dough hook. Mix until a cohesive dough is formed and the dough pulls away from the sides of the bowl. The dough should be just slightly sticky.

2. Add more flour by the teaspoonful if needed, but keep the dough as soft as possible. If the dough is too dry, add a little water.

3. Once the dough is cohesive, knead for another 5 minutes, either by hand or with the mixer. Cover the bowl with a damp kitchen towel and let it stand for 20 minutes.

MAKE PASTA BY HAND

1. Mound the flour on a clean work surface. Make a well in the middle of the flour with steep sides.

2. Break the eggs into the well. Add the salt and olive oil and gently mix together with a fork. Gradually start incorporating the flour by pulling in the flour from the sides of the well, but try to maintain the integrity of the well as long as possible. Usually this finally gives way into a shaggy mess when about half of the flour has been mixed in.

3. With your hands or a bench scraper, continue working the dough until it comes together. If the dough is too dry, add a little water; if too wet or sticky, add a little flour.

4. Begin kneading the dough and keep kneading until it becomes smooth and elastic, about 8–10 minutes. Cover with a damp kitchen towel and let it rest for 20 minutes.

SHAPE YOUR PASTA

1. To roll by hand, divide your dough into two pieces, keeping one covered to prevent it from drying out.

2. On a large floured work area, flatten the dough into a disk. Working from the center at all times, use a rolling pin to flatten the disk out from the center to the outer edge. With each roll, rotate the dough one-quarter turn and flip the dough over once or twice to ensure the dough is not sticking.

3. Roll out the dough to about ¹⁄₁₆" thick (about half the thickness of a penny). If the dough springs back as you are rolling, cover it with a damp towel and let it sit for an additional 10 minutes.

4. Once the dough is rolled thin, dust it with flour; then fold it in half lengthwise. Dust and fold in half again in the same direction so you end up with a long rectangular sheet of pasta in four layers.

5. Using a very sharp, large knife, slice the sheet of dough into strips as wide as your desired pasta: for spaghetti, cut very thin strips; for tagliatelle, cut ½" strips; and for lasagna, cut 3" strips.

6. Set the strips on floured tea towels or drape them over a long broom handle, being careful not to let the pieces touch if at all possible.

7. If you would like to use this dough for macaroni, penne, or other tube pastas, use a pasta extruder. After mixing the dough and letting it rest, extrude the pasta into your desired shape and lay on floured tea towels.

COOKING AND STORING THE PASTA

1. To cook the fresh pasta, bring a pot of salted water to a boil. Add the fresh pasta and cook for approximately 2 minutes. Fresh pasta reaches the al dente stage very quickly, so be ready.

2. To store the pasta, let the strips or tubes dry for several hours, turning them if necessary to dry thoroughly. You may also dry them in your food dehydrator for 2–4 hours at 135°F. When they are dry, place them in airtight packages and store for up to 1 year. Alternatively, flour the strips to keep them from sticking, place them in freezer-safe bags, and freeze them for up to 1 month.

Soba Noodles

Buckwheat is the true gluten- and grain-free flour, as it isn't wheat at all. It's actually a seed that's in the same family as rhubarb and sorrel! The problem when making noodles, however, is that gluten is what makes any dough stay cohesive and elastic rather than crumble. Thus, one technique Japanese masters employ when working with 100 percent buckwheat dough is to use boiling water to gelatinize the seed flour to help it bind. Also, if you don't need to have a gluten-free noodle, feel free to use 80 percent buckwheat and 20 percent all-purpose flour, as that will help the noodles soften and bind as well.

HANDS-ON: 30 minutes

INACTIVE: none

READY IN: 30 minutes

DIFFICULTY LEVEL: ★ ★

YIELD: Serves 4; Makes 2 pounds cooked pasta

COST PER SERVING: $ $

GF

CALORIES: 201

FAT: 2 g

PROTEIN: 8 g

SODIUM: 7 mg

FIBER: 6 g

CARBOHYDRATES: 42 g

SUGAR: 2 g

2 cups buckwheat flour
½ cup boiling water
Buckwheat flour, tapioca starch, or arrowroot powder, for rolling

1. Place the flour in the bowl of an electric mixer fitted with the dough hook and whisk it once or twice to sift it.

2. Pour the boiling water over and turn the mixer on low. Knead it until it comes together into a rough and slightly crumbly dough. If the dough feels dry or you can still see dry flour after a few minutes of kneading, then add water a tablespoon at a time until the dough holds together. Conversely, if the dough feels wet or sticky, add more flour a tablespoon at a time until it becomes a workable dough and is no longer sticky.

3. Continue kneading until the dough holds together easily, does not crack while kneading, and becomes smooth, about 5–6 minutes. Resist the urge to add more flour at this point. The dough will be very dense, but should be soft, smooth, and not at all sticky.

4. Dust a flat work surface with starch or buckwheat flour and flatten the ball into a ½"-thick disk. Dust the work surface and the dough again.

5. Roll out the dough out from the center into as thin a sheet as possible, preferably less than ⅛" thick. Dust with more starch or flour as needed to keep the dough from sticking and flip it over at times, if needed.

6. Once the dough is rolled thin, dust it with flour; then fold it in half lengthwise. Dust and fold in half again in the same direction so you end up with a long rectangular sheet of pasta in four layers. Using a very sharp large knife, slice the sheet of dough into thin strips; then unfurl them into noodles.

7. Cover your pile of finished noodles with a slightly damp tea towel as you continue to cut, as buckwheat noodles dry out very quickly.

8. To cook the noodles right away, bring a large pot of water to a boil; then toss in several tablespoons of salt and the cut noodles. Stir to prevent sticking and boil for about 1–2 minutes.

9. To store the noodles for later use, the uncooked noodles may be frozen for up to 3 months, or you may dehydrate them in a food dehydrator for 1–3 hours at 135°F; then store them in an airtight container for up to 4 months.

Taco Shells

Making hard taco shells needn't be difficult. All you need to do is form them and dry them out, which can be done surprisingly easily in a regular kitchen oven.

HANDS-ON: 15 minutes

INACTIVE: none

READY IN: 15 minutes

DIFFICULTY LEVEL: ★

YIELD: Serves 6; Makes 12 taco shells

COST PER SERVING: $ $

GF   V   V   DF   EF

CALORIES: 105

FAT: 1 g

PROTEIN: 3 g

SODIUM: 22 mg

FIBER: 3 g

CARBOHYDRATES: 21 g

SUGAR: 0 g

12 corn tortillas

1. Preheat the oven to 200°F.

2. First, steam and warm the tortillas by laying the tortillas in an overlapping pattern on a barely moist cotton sack, dishtowel, or tea towel. Pull the ends of the towel up over the tortillas to enclose them; then place the towel on a baking sheet and set in the oven to warm for 5 minutes.

3. Remove the tortillas and increase the oven to 375°F. Keep the tortillas wrapped—you want them to be soft, warm, and pliable.

4. When the oven is fully preheated, drape each tortilla over two bars of the top oven rack so that the sides hang down, placing one row in the front and one row in the back, if possible. Bake until crispy but not brown, 6–8 minutes.

5. To serve immediately, stuff with your favorite taco fillings, or to store them, place the taco shells in an airtight container or plastic bag and set them aside for up to 2 days.

Peanut Butter

You can most certainly make peanut butter just from peanuts—in fact, the best nut butters are simply that: nuts ground up into a spreadable butter. The coconut oil in this recipe makes for a very thick, smooth peanut butter, but you can certainly adjust the recipe to your own personal tastes. For that "store-bought flavor," plain peanuts have a less complex, earthier flavor and are far superior for this use.

HANDS-ON: 20 minutes

INACTIVE: none

READY IN: 20 minutes

DIFFICULTY LEVEL: ★ ★

YIELD: Serves 8; Makes 2 cups

COST PER SERVING: $ $

GF V DF EF

CALORIES: 260

FAT: 23 g

PROTEIN: 9 g

SODIUM: 302 mg

FIBER: 3 g

CARBOHYDRATES: 8 g

SUGAR: 4 g

2 cups peanuts, shelled and skinned
1 teaspoon unrefined sea salt
3 teaspoons raw honey or whole cane sugar
½ teaspoon blackstrap molasses
2 tablespoons coconut oil
1 tablespoon peanut oil

1. For a deeper flavor, first roast the peanuts by laying them on a baking sheet and roasting them in a 400°F oven for 10–12 minutes, shaking halfway through. Pull them out just as they begin to brown. Do not let them burn, or your peanut butter will be bitter. Cool to room temperature.

2. Place all ingredients in a food processor or mortar and grind until you have reached your desired texture, about 4–6 minutes.

3. Store in an airtight container for 3–4 weeks in the cupboard, or in the refrigerator for 3–4 months.

Chocolate Hazelnut Spread

The best part about this recipe, apart from how ridiculously easy it is to make and the rich, creamy, nutty flavor, is that you can control the amount of sugar that you add. Also, it is definitely worth it to find hazelnuts that are already blanched and peeled. Otherwise, be prepared to put on your favorite music and make an evening of it.

HANDS-ON: 10 minutes

INACTIVE: none

READY IN: 10 minutes

DIFFICULTY LEVEL: ★

YIELD: Serves 12; Makes 3 cups

COST PER SERVING: $ $

CALORIES: 341

FAT: 25 g

PROTEIN: 7 g

SODIUM: 100 mg

FIBER: 5 g

CARBOHYDRATES: 29 g

SUGAR: 22 g

4 cups (1 pound) blanched hazelnuts

2 cups powdered sugar

⅔ cup cocoa powder

¼ cup hazelnut, walnut, or coconut oil, plus more as needed

1 tablespoon vanilla extract

½ teaspoon salt

1. Grind the hazelnuts in a food processor until they start to look like peanut butter, about 2–4 minutes.

2. Add the powdered sugar, cocoa powder, hazelnut oil, vanilla extract, and salt. Continue to process, adding more hazelnut oil a few tablespoons at a time, until the mixture becomes very smooth.

3. Store in an airtight container for up to 6 weeks at room temperature.

French-Fried Onions

If you need to be grain-free, feel free to skip the breading altogether, as these will still crisp up quite nicely. Be sure to rinse and drain the onion strands thoroughly after soaking them in the milk if you skip the dredging.

HANDS-ON: 20 minutes

INACTIVE: 30 minutes

READY IN: 1 hour

DIFFICULTY LEVEL: ★ ★

YIELD: Serves 8; Makes 4 cups

COST PER SERVING: $

GF V DF EF

CALORIES: 821

FAT: 79 g

PROTEIN: 5 g

SODIUM: 322 mg

FIBER: 1 g

CARBOHYDRATES: 23 g

SUGAR: 4 g

1 large onion

2 cups milk or buttermilk

1½ cups flour (any variety, including gluten-free varieties)

1 teaspoon unrefined sea salt

Black pepper, to taste

⅛ teaspoon cayenne pepper or smoked paprika

2–3 cups palm shortening, lard, tallow, or your favorite deep-frying oil (enough to have about 2" of heated oil in your pot)

1. Peel the onion; then slice it paper-thin. Separate all the onion strands and layer them in a wide bowl or shallow baking dish. Pour the milk over and let them sit for 20–30 minutes.

2. Meanwhile, sift the spices into the flour in a large bowl and heat the oil over medium-high heat until it's hot. (If you slip one onion strand in, it should bubble vigorously without splattering. On a thermometer it's about 375°F.)

3. Working in small batches, grab a handful of onion strands from the bowl, shake off the excess milk, dredge them in the flour, shake off the excess flour, and then drop them into the hot oil. Stir lightly to keep them from sticking. Remove when they're golden brown, 2–3 minutes.

4. Drain on paper towels and use immediately. Store in an airtight container at room temperature for up to 3 days.

Pasta Sauce

You can't go wrong with this traditional pasta sauce, and it's highly customizable to fit your needs. Even better, it takes only a few minutes to get everything in the pot, and then as it simmers for a number of hours, your house will smell fantastic! Also, feel free to add lots of finely shredded vegetables in with the tomatoes if you like to have a more "garden-style" pasta sauce—carrots, zucchini, and fennel are common favorites. If you're looking to replicate the flavor of some of the big-name brands of pasta sauce, you'll want to triple the amount of sugar called for here and add ½ teaspoon of citric acid.

HANDS-ON: 20 minutes

INACTIVE: 2–6 hours

READY IN: 6 hours

DIFFICULTY LEVEL: ★ ★

YIELD: Serves 4; Makes 2 quarts

COST PER SERVING: $ $ $

GF   V   DF   EF

CALORIES: 164

FAT: 1 g

PROTEIN: 5 g

SODIUM: 1,855 mg

FIBER: 8 g

CARBOHYDRATES: 38 g

SUGAR: 20 g

1 pound ground beef or Italian sausage (optional)

3 tablespoons butter or olive oil (optional)

1 large onion, chopped

2 celery stalks, finely chopped

2 bell peppers, finely chopped

6 garlic cloves, minced

2 teaspoons sea salt

¼ cup cornstarch or arrowroot powder

1 quart stewed whole or diced tomatoes, drained

2 cups tomato sauce

1 cup red wine (optional)

¼ cup dried basil

2 tablespoons dried oregano

2 tablespoons dried parsley

2 tablespoons unrefined cane sugar

1. Brown the meat over medium heat until no longer pink. Do not drain fat unless the meat begins to stew rather than sear due to the volume of fat.

2. Toss in the onion, celery, peppers, garlic, and salt, along with any other vegetables you choose to use. Sauté until the onions and celery are soft and translucent but not brown, 7–8 minutes.

3. Toss in the starch and stir to combine. Add the stewed tomatoes, tomato sauce, wine, herbs, and sugar. Bring to a steady simmer; then reduce heat to low and cover. Simmer for 2–6 hours, stirring occasionally.

4. For a very smooth sauce, purée with a stick blender.

5. Store in the refrigerator for up to 3 days, or in the freezer for up to 6 months.

Pizza Sauce

Having an all-natural pizza sauce on hand makes pulling together a pizza quickly a breeze. If you freeze it, consider freezing it in small batches so that you only have to thaw enough for one pizza at a time.

HANDS-ON: 5 minutes

INACTIVE: 30 minutes

READY IN: 35 minutes

DIFFICULTY LEVEL: ★

YIELD: Serves 8; Makes 1 quart

COST PER SERVING: $

CALORIES: 52

FAT: 2 g

PROTEIN: 2 g

SODIUM: 175 mg

FIBER: 2 g

CARBOHYDRATES: 8 g

SUGAR: 6 g

1 tablespoon olive oil

6 cloves garlic, minced

1 tablespoon dried oregano

2 tablespoons dried basil

4 cups tomato sauce

1 teaspoon whole cane sugar

½ teaspoon salt

1. Heat the olive oil over medium heat; then sauté the garlic until it is fragrant, about 30 seconds.

2. Add dried herbs and stir; then pour in the tomato sauce. Sprinkle the sugar and the salt over the sauce.

3. Reduce temperature to medium-low and simmer uncovered for 30 minutes.

4. Store in an airtight container in the refrigerator for up to 3 days, and in the freezer for up to 6 months.

Tomato Sauce

Tomatoes are great summer crops! They are delightful served fresh in a salad or sandwiched between fresh basil and mozzarella in the typical Caprese style. They're also fantastic for cooking all year round. They keep their flavor well and allow you to make big batches of tomato sauce to freeze, which you can then thaw through the winter for tomato soup or any recipe that calls for tomato sauce or tomato paste.

HANDS-ON: 10 minutes

INACTIVE: 4 hours

READY IN: 4 hours

DIFFICULTY LEVEL: ★

YIELD: Serves 12; Makes 3 cups

COST PER SERVING: $

GF V V DF EF

CALORIES: 81

FAT: 1 g

PROTEIN: 4 g

SODIUM: 22 mg

FIBER: 5 g

CARBOHYDRATES: 18 g

SUGAR: 12 g

12 pounds tomatoes (Roma-type are best, but any tomato will work just fine)

1½ teaspoons sea salt (optional)

1. Quarter tomatoes and place in a large, heavy-bottomed stockpot. You may blanch and peel the tomatoes first if you'd like, but it's much quicker and yields a deeper, richer sauce to leave the skins on. Add salt if desired—I prefer to skip the salt now to give greater variety later. I have found if I add the salt now and then add salt again when I make the pasta sauce or soup, it's overpowering.

2. Add a few tablespoons of water, cover, and heat over medium heat for 15–20 minutes, until the tomatoes start to really release their juices. Remove the cover and decrease heat to medium-low. Simmer gently for 3–4 hours, stirring occasionally toward the end to make sure the tomatoes don't stick to the bottom of the pan.

3. Remove the pan from the heat when the sauce is the desired consistency. Process through a food mill to make it smooth. If you don't have a food mill, the mixture can be pressed through a fine sieve with the back of a spoon as well, but it will take much longer. Freeze the sauce and compost the leftover skins. The sauce will keep in the freezer for up to 6 months.

TOMATO PASTE

For tomato paste, follow the recipe for Tomato Sauce, but add an additional 1 hour to the cook time. This will decrease the yield to approximately 2 cups.

Worcestershire Sauce

No kitchen is complete without a bottle of this ubiquitous salty, savory sauce on hand!

HANDS-ON: 20 minutes

INACTIVE: none

READY IN: 20 minutes

DIFFICULTY LEVEL: ★ ★ ★

YIELD: Serves 24; Makes 1½ cups

COST PER SERVING: $ $

GF DF EF

CALORIES: 33

FAT: 1 g

PROTEIN: 1 g

SODIUM: 57 mg

FIBER: 0 g

CARBOHYDRATES: 5 g

SUGAR: 4 g

½ cup malt vinegar

½ cup apple cider vinegar

½ cup blackstrap molasses

4 tablespoons fermented fish sauce

2 tablespoons tamarind paste

1 tablespoon soy sauce (optional)

3 tablespoons onion juice, or 1 teaspoon dehydrated onion

1 teaspoon black pepper

½ teaspoon cinnamon

½ teaspoon ground cloves

¼ teaspoon cayenne pepper

2 tablespoons olive oil

2 shallots, finely minced

4 cloves garlic, finely minced

1 teaspoon freshly grated gingerroot

8 anchovies, minced

Juice of 1 lime

1. Whisk together the vinegars, molasses, fish sauce, tamarind paste, soy sauce, and onion juice. Set aside.

2. Preheat a small, dry sauté pan over medium heat. Toast the spices until fragrant, about 1 minute. Pour into a small bowl and set aside.

3. In a small saucepan, heat the oil over medium heat; then sauté the shallots until transparent and beginning to brown, 2–3 minutes. Add garlic, ginger, anchovies, and reserved spices and continue to sauté just until fragrant, about 30 seconds.

4. Pour in the vinegar mixture and scrape up any bits on the bottom of the pan. Bring to a full simmer; then remove from the heat and let cool completely.

5. Strain through a fine-mesh strainer into a bowl and stir in the lime juice. Pour into a jar or bottle for long-term storage. Will keep in the refrigerator for 1–2 months.

Stock

Homemade stocks are extremely nutritious and provide you with copious amounts of needed minerals. As with any stock, the longer you simmer it, the more nutritious the final stock will be. The only thing to keep in mind is that with every stock, there's a fine line between pulling every bit of nutritious goodness out of the ingredients and cooking it so long that it starts to taste "off." Follow the guidelines in each specific recipe and taste your own stocks periodically while cooking, as various stoves can cook at wildly different rates. Also, you may wonder about the vinegar in some of the recipes. The vinegar is present in all of the stocks made from bones in order to increase the amount of minerals in the stock. Bones are—very literally— a storehouse of minerals in the body. Just think of what an important role calcium plays in bone health! Thus, we're wanting to get as many minerals as possible out of the bones and into the stock, and vinegar helps promote that transfer. If you'd prefer to leave it out, feel free to do so. (And if you skip the vinegar, you can also skip the one-hour soaking period at the beginning of each recipe.)

Beef Stock

HANDS-ON: 15 minutes

INACTIVE: 1–2 days

READY IN: 2 days

DIFFICULTY LEVEL: ★ ★

YIELD: Serves 24; Makes 6 quarts

COST PER SERVING: $

GF DF EF

CALORIES: 31

FAT: 1 g

PROTEIN: 4 g

SODIUM: 11 mg

FIBER: 0 g

CARBOHYDRATES: 3 g

SUGAR: 1 g

5–6 pounds beef bones

Enough water to completely cover the bones by at least 1", usually about 6 quarts

1 tablespoon vinegar

2 carrots, cut into 2–3" pieces

4 stalks of celery, cut into 2–3" pieces

1 medium yellow onion, peeled and quartered

2 leeks, sliced lengthwise and cut into 2–3" pieces

2–3 bay leaves

1 tablespoon black peppercorns

1 large handful fresh parsley

1. Rinse and clean the bones under running water. Pat them dry.

2. Roast the bones at 400°F for 45–60 minutes, until the bones are well browned. Drain off any fat.

3. Place the bones in a large stockpot. Cover with water and add in the vinegar. Let sit for 1 hour.

4. Add chopped vegetables, bay leaves, and peppercorns; then bring the water to a boil. Once boiling, reduce to a very gentle simmer and simmer uncovered.

5. Check the stock every half-hour for the first hour or two to skim off any foam and double-check that the stock is simmering (if heat is too low, stock will be hot but not show any movement).

6. Cover and continue to simmer for 24–48 hours, adding water as needed to keep the bones submerged.

7. When you are ready to finish the stock, toss in the parsley and let simmer for a final 10–15 minutes.

8. Filter through a fine-mesh sieve and pour into storage containers.

9. Refrigerate for up to 5 days, or freeze for up to 1 year.

Chicken Stock

HANDS ON: 10 minutes

INACTIVE: 8–12 hours

READY IN: 12 hours

DIFFICULTY LEVEL: ★

YIELD: Serves 24; Makes 6 quarts

COST PER SERVING: $

GF DF EF

CALORIES: 38

FAT: 1 g

PROTEIN: 4 g

SODIUM: 15 mg

FIBER: 0 g

CARBOHYDRATES: 3 g

SUGAR: 0 g

2 pounds chicken bones, or 1 chicken carcass

Enough water to completely cover the bones by at least 1", usually about 6 quarts

1 tablespoon vinegar

1 carrot, cut into 2–3" pieces

3 stalks of celery, cut into 2–3" pieces

1 onion, peeled and quartered

2–3 bay leaves

1 tablespoon black peppercorns

1 large handful fresh parsley

1. Place chicken bones or carcass in a large stockpot. Cover with water and add in the vinegar. Let sit for 1 hour.

2. Add chopped vegetables, bay leaves, and peppercorns; then bring the water to a boil. Once boiling, reduce to a very gentle simmer, uncovered.

3. Check the stock every half-hour for the first hour or two to skim off any foam and double-check that the stock is simmering (if heat is too low, stock will be hot but not show any movement).

4. Cover and continue to simmer for 12–18 hours, adding water as needed to keep the bones submerged.

5. When you are ready to finish the stock, toss in the parsley and let simmer for a final 10–15 minutes.

6. Filter through a fine-mesh sieve and pour into storage containers.

7. Refrigerate for up to 5 days, or freeze for up to 1 year.

Vegetable or Mushroom Stock

The beautiful thing about a vegetable stock is you can vary the ingredients completely according to what you have on hand and vary the amounts according to your tastes. I often refer to this as "clean out the refrigerator stock." If you want a mushroom stock that makes risottos, beef stroganoff, and lasagna taste out of this world, double the mushrooms in this recipe and add in 4 ounces of dried shiitake or porcini mushrooms along with the peppers.

HANDS-ON: 20 minutes

INACTIVE: 1 hour

READY IN: 1 hour

DIFFICULTY LEVEL: ★

YIELD: Serves 24; Makes 6 quarts

COST PER SERVING: $

CALORIES: 47

FAT: 2 g

PROTEIN: 1 g

SODIUM: 34 mg

FIBER: 2 g

CARBOHYDRATES: 6 g

SUGAR: 3 g

4 tablespoons clarified butter or olive oil

3 onions, coarsely chopped, skins reserved

8 stalks celery, coarsely chopped

6 carrots, coarsely chopped

2 leeks, sliced lengthwise and coarsely chopped (optional)

1 pound mushrooms, any variety, halved (optional)

8 large garlic cloves, with skins, smashed

6 quarts fresh water

2 bell peppers, cut into wide strips

2 sprigs fresh thyme

4 bay leaves

1 tablespoon black peppercorns

1 large handful fresh parsley

1. Melt the butter in a large stockpot over medium-high heat. Toss in the onions, celery, carrots, leeks, and mushrooms and stir to coat. Cook, stirring occasionally, until all vegetables have begun to caramelize, 15–20 minutes. Add the garlic and continue to brown for another 2–3 minutes.

2. Pour in the water and bring to a boil. Once boiling, reduce to a very gentle simmer and add in the peppers, thyme, bay leaves, peppercorns, and reserved onion skins.

3. Simmer, covered, for 30–60 minutes, until the stock is very aromatic.

4. When you are ready to finish the stock, toss in the parsley and let simmer for a final 5–10 minutes.

5. Filter through a fine-mesh sieve and pour into storage containers.

6. Refrigerate for up to 5 days, or freeze for up to 1 year.

Fish Stock

Any whitefish makes a delicious stock, but avoid oily fish, such as salmon.

HANDS-ON: 20 minutes

INACTIVE: 3–6 hours

READY IN: 3 hours

DIFFICULTY LEVEL: ★

YIELD: Serves 16; Makes 4 quarts

COST PER SERVING: $

 GF DF EF

CALORIES: 39 g

FAT: 1 g

PROTEIN: 5 g

SODIUM: 12 mg

FIBER: 0 g

CARBOHYDRATES: 0 g

SUGAR: 0 g

4 tablespoons clarified butter or olive oil

6 celery stalks, coarsely chopped

2 onions, quartered

2 carrots, coarsely chopped

4 pounds fish bones (including heads, if possible)

1 cup white wine

4 quarts hot water

1 teaspoon black peppercorns

8 sprigs fresh thyme

2 dried bay leaves

1 large handful fresh parsley

1. In a large, heavy-bottomed stockpot, melt the butter over medium-high heat, toss in the celery, onions, and carrots, and toss to coat. Sauté until just beginning to brown, 8–10 minutes; then add the fish bones and the wine.

2. Cover and let simmer until the fish bones are white and no longer opaque, 5–10 minutes.

3. Add the hot water and bring just to a simmer—do not boil. As soon as it begins to simmer, turn the heat to low and add the peppercorns, thyme, and bay leaves. Cover and simmer for 3–6 hours. Skim off any impurities that float to the surface.

4. When you are ready to finish the stock, toss in the parsley and let simmer for a final 5–10 minutes.

5. Filter through a fine-mesh sieve and pour into storage containers.

6. Refrigerate for up to 5 days, or freeze for up to 1 year.

Shrimp Stock

You can make this stock with any crustacean, such as lobster or crayfish.

HANDS-ON: 20 minutes

INACTIVE: 20–30 minutes

READY IN: 1 hour

DIFFICULTY LEVEL: ★

YIELD: Serves 4; Makes 1 quart

COST PER SERVING: $ $

CALORIES: 193

FAT: 8 g

PROTEIN: 24 g

SODIUM: 196 mg

FIBER: 1 g

CARBOHYDRATES: 6 g

SUGAR: 2 g

2 tablespoons butter

Shrimp shells from 1 pound of shrimp

6 cups cold water

1 bell pepper, cut into large strips

2 stalks celery, coarsely chopped

1 onion, quartered

2–3 cloves garlic, coarsely chopped

4–5 stems fresh parsley

1 teaspoon lemon juice

1. In a heavy-bottomed stockpot, melt the butter over medium-high heat and sauté the shrimp shells until they turn completely pink, 2–3 minutes.

2. Pour in the cold water, add the vegetables and garlic, and return to a boil. Reduce heat to a gentle simmer, cover, and simmer for 20–30 minutes, until the stock is very aromatic. Toss in the parsley and simmer uncovered for an additional 5 minutes.

3. Strain through a fine-mesh strainer to remove the solids and stir in the lemon juice.

4. Store in an airtight container in the refrigerator for up to 3 days, or in the freezer for 5–6 months.

Bean Broth

Bean broth is an easy, frugal way to have a flavorful broth that can be used in anything that needs a hearty, rich flavor. It's great for vegetarians or anyone who wants to stretch the grocery budget without sacrificing satiety or flavor.

HANDS-ON: 20 minutes

INACTIVE: 21 hours

READY IN: 21 hours

DIFFICULTY LEVEL: ★

YIELD: Serves 8; Makes 2 quarts

COST PER SERVING: $

CALORIES: 280

FAT: 1 g

PROTEIN: 16 g

SODIUM: 922 mg

FIBER: 12 g

CARBOHYDRATES: 51 g

SUGAR: 4 g

3 cups dried pinto beans, navy beans, or your favorite bean

¼ cup vinegar

12 cups water

3 onions, coarsely chopped

12 cloves garlic, crushed

4 stalks celery, coarsely chopped

1 dried chipotle pepper, left whole (optional)

3 teaspoons sea salt

1½ teaspoons black pepper

1. Place beans in a large bowl and cover with at least 2" of warm water. Pour in the vinegar and stir. Let sit for 12–18 hours; then pour off the soaking liquid and rinse the beans.

2. Add beans to a large stockpot and add the 12 cups water, along with the onions, garlic, celery, and dried chipotle. Bring to a boil over medium-high heat; then reduce temperature to medium-low, cover, and simmer until beans are tender, about 3 hours. Add salt and pepper and adjust seasonings to taste.

3. Strain the beans, remove the vegetables, and reserve for other uses—salads, chili, bean dips, or refried beans, for example.

4. Pour the broth into storage containers. Store in the refrigerator for up to 5 days, or freeze for up to 1 year.

Vegetable Broth Powder

Store-bought bouillon cubes and broth powders are notorious for containing monosodium glutamate (MSG), the excitotoxin that can cause a host of physical, behavioral, and emotional issues ranging from headaches and ringing in the ears to ADHD and inability to control anger in young children. By making this homemade broth powder, you can have a natural flavor enhancer to add to soups and sauces that is nourishing, easy to make, and easy to use, not to mention delicious. Despite containing only vegetables, herbs, salt, and nutritional yeast, this broth powder is a dead ringer for chicken bouillon and it just may become your new secret ingredient for making all your dishes more flavorful!

HANDS-ON: 5 minutes

INACTIVE: none

READY IN: 5 minutes

DIFFICULTY LEVEL: ★

YIELD: Serves 72; Makes 1½ cups

COST PER SERVING: $

CALORIES: 7

FAT: 0 g

PROTEIN: 1 g

SODIUM: 341 mg

FIBER: 0 g

CARBOHYDRATES: 1 g

SUGAR: 0 g

1 cup nutritional yeast

⅛ cup sea salt

1½ tablespoons onion powder

½ teaspoon garlic powder

½ tablespoon turmeric

1 tablespoon dried dill

½ teaspoon celery seed

½ teaspoon dried basil

1 teaspoon powdered thyme

1 tablespoon dried parsley

½ teaspoon dehydrated peppers (optional)

½ teaspoon dried lovage (optional)

1. Place all the ingredients in a blender and blend until homogeneous.

2. To make broth or to use in soups, stews, and sauces, use 1 scant teaspoon of powder for every cup of water.

Pesto

Pesto is incredibly easy and fairly quick if you make it in a food processor, but the best flavor will come if you chop everything by hand. It takes a few extra minutes, but trust me, it's worth it. Because you add the ingredients a bit at a time, some items end up chopped into oblivion and some are left a bit chunky. This means more variation in flavor and texture as you chew, which is basically my definition of "soul-satisfyingly delicious." Basil and pine nuts are the universal standard, but feel free to use any dark leafy green (spinach, arugula, parsley) and any nut (walnuts, pecans, cashews) for flavor variations.

HANDS-ON: 10 minutes

INACTIVE: none

READY IN: 10 minutes

DIFFICULTY LEVEL: ★

YIELD: Serves 4; Makes 1 cup

COST PER SERVING: $ $ $

GF V EF

CALORIES: 360

FAT: 36 g

PROTEIN: 7 g

SODIUM: 134 mg

FIBER: 3 g

CARBOHYDRATES: 7 g

SUGAR: 0 g

1 large bunch of basil, stems removed
3 large cloves garlic, peeled and very coarsely chopped
¾ cup raw pine nuts
4–5 tablespoons extra-virgin olive oil
1 ounce Parmesan cheese, grated (approximately ¼ cup)

1. If using a food processor, place basil, garlic, and pine nuts in it and pulse several times until everything is finely chopped.

2. With the motor running, pour in the olive oil.

3. Scrape down the sides; then add in the cheese and pulse to combine.

4. If crafting pesto by hand, begin by chopping the garlic and about a quarter of the basil. Once these are fairly coarsely chopped, add 2–3 more basil leaves, chop, and continue to add basil a few leaves at a time until the basil is all incorporated and very finely minced.

5. Add about half the pine nuts and chop them coarsely. Add the rest of the pine nuts; then chop those coarsely as well.

6. Add half of the Parmesan and chop until it's coarsely chopped. Add the rest of the Parmesan and chop until everything is finely minced.

7. Press the pesto into a disk and place in a very small bowl. Cover with the olive oil and reserve. Stir together just before serving. To store, cover with plastic wrap and place in the refrigerator for up to 24 hours.

CHOPPING TIP

Be sure to use a very sharp chef's knife or mezzaluna. Otherwise, you'll just be shredding the basil rather than cutting it, and chopping the pine nuts will become a frustrating chore.

Homemade Extracts

Making your own extracts is extremely easy—it just takes 6–9 months. The flavor is strong, though, once the extract is finished and oh-so-worth-the-wait.

HANDS-ON: 5 minutes

INACTIVE: 6–9 months

READY IN: 9 months

DIFFICULTY LEVEL: ★

YIELD: Serves 84; Makes 2 cups

COST PER SERVING: $

CALORIES: 15

FAT: 0 g

PROTEIN: 0 g

SODIUM: 3 mg

FIBER: 0 g

CARBOHYDRATES: 0 g

SUGAR: 0 g

2 cups vodka (80 proof at least)

3 cups flavoring (cacao beans, mint leaves, etc.)

1. For any extract, fill a 1-quart Mason jar about two-thirds full with your flavoring; then top it off with vodka.

2. Place in a cool, dark place where it will not be disturbed. Once every week in the first 2 months, shake the jar, but other than that, just let it sit. After 6 months, taste it to see if the flavor has developed. If yes, strain it and place it into bottles. If no, leave it for 3 more months and check the flavor again at the 9-month mark.

VARIATIONS

Vanilla: Use 10–20 vanilla beans.

Lemon: Fill the jar halfway with lemon zest (not the pith). You may want to make a smaller batch of this one, since zest is difficult to come by.

Peppermint: Loosely pack the jar with mint leaves and top off with vodka.

Chocolate: Fill the jar two-thirds of the way with cacao beans.

Coffee: Fill the jar two-thirds of the way with coffee beans.

Sweetened Condensed Milk

It's just as it sounds: milk that has been sweetened, then condensed. Give it a bit of time and it's about the easiest recipe you'll ever make. An absolutely crucial part of this recipe is heating the milk on the absolutely lowest setting possible, unless you want to whisk constantly for the hour or two it takes to reduce!

HANDS-ON: 25 minutes

INACTIVE: 2 hours

READY IN: 2 hours

DIFFICULTY LEVEL: ★ ★ ★

YIELD: Serves 6; Makes 1½ cups

COST PER SERVING: $ $

  EF

CALORIES: 172

FAT: 6 g

PROTEIN: 3 g

SODIUM: 36 mg

FIBER: 0 g

CARBOHYDRATES: 26 g

SUGAR: 27 g

2 cups whole milk
⅔ cup unrefined cane sugar
2 tablespoons butter
1 teaspoon vanilla extract

1. Heat the milk and sugar in a large saucepan over medium-low heat until the milk is steaming. Stir until the sugar is fully dissolved; then reduce heat to low and let it steam until it is reduced to about half its original volume, about 2 hours. You may choose to remove the skin every so often if you wish, or if it's raw milk, stir it back in, but doing so is completely optional.

2. When the milk and sugar mixture has reduced, whisk in the butter and vanilla, remove from heat, and then let cool completely. The milk will continue to thicken slightly as it cools.

3. Store in the refrigerator for 2–3 weeks.

Evaporated Milk

If you flip over a can of evaporated milk, you'll realize that it isn't just milk. Partially hydrogenated soybean oil, carrageenan, and four different preservatives accompany the milk, so the homemade version is definitely superior from a health standpoint. And why on earth would you want to use evaporated milk in the first place? Why not just use milk or cream, if you need something thicker? Well, evaporated milk gives the thickness of cream with the lighter mouthfeel of milk due to the different fat content, so it's more versatile for favorites like eggnog, homemade cream of mushroom soup, and stovetop macaroni and cheese. Simple, simple, simple! Evaporated milk is merely milk that has been reduced to about 40 percent of its original amount, making for a much thicker, richer option.

HANDS-ON: 15 minutes	
INACTIVE: 2–3 hours	
READY-IN: 3 hours	
DIFFICULTY LEVEL: ★ ★ ★	
YIELD: Serves 4; Makes 1 cup	
COST PER SERVING: $	

GF

CALORIES: 93	
FAT: 5 g	
PROTEIN: 5 g	
SODIUM: 66 mg	
FIBER: 0 g	
CARBOHYDRATES: 7 g	
SUGAR: 8 g	

2½ cups whole milk

1. Pour milk into a wide saucepan or skillet. Heat milk over medium-low heat to bring it to a temperature where it can evaporate easily, but do not let it boil, as the milk will curdle. Once it's steaming, reduce heat to low and let it sit on the stovetop uncovered until it's reduced to about 1 cup, about 2–3 hours; then remove and cool. You may stir occasionally, if desired, or remove the skin that forms on the top, but be careful not to scrape up any milk from the bottom or sides of the pan.

2. Store in the refrigerator for 2–3 weeks.

Applesauce

HANDS-ON: 20 minutes

INACTIVE: 1 hour

READY IN: 1½ hours

DIFFICULTY LEVEL: ★

YIELD: Serves 6; Makes 1½ quarts

COST PER SERVING: $ $ $

CALORIES: 143

FAT: 0 mg

PROTEIN: 1 g

SODIUM: 0 g

FIBER: 4 g

CARBOHYDRATES: 38 g

SUGAR: 30 g

Applesauce is a great addition to any pantry because it can do so many different things. It can be a sweet treat during the day, breakfast when set next to waffles, and even better when drizzled over pork. It also easily adds sweetness and moisture as a baking substitute for those who want to avoid sugar and eat more healthily.

4 pounds apples

1. Wash, cut, and quarter 4 pounds of apples. Don't worry about stemming or seeding them.

2. Place the pieces in a large stockpot and toss in a few tablespoons of water to keep them from burning. Set pot over medium heat and once it comes to a boil, reduce the heat to medium-low and simmer uncovered until the apples are very soft, about 1 hour.

3. Pass the remaining applesauce through a food sieve to remove the stems, peels, and seeds, and enjoy!

4. Store in an airtight container in the refrigerator for up to 1 week, or in the freezer for up to 6 months.

Cranberry Sauce

HANDS-ON: 5 minutes

INACTIVE: 10 minutes

READY IN: 15 minutes

DIFFICULTY LEVEL: ★

YIELD: Serves 4; Makes 2½ cups

COST PER SERVING: $ $

CALORIES: 181

FAT: 0 g

PROTEIN: 0 g

SODIUM: 4 mg

FIBER: 3 g

CARBOHYDRATES: 47 g

SUGAR: 41 g

This basic cranberry sauce is the traditional sauce you'll find on holiday tables, but you can also use it year-round as a base for sauces to accompany pork and chicken.

3 cups fresh or frozen cranberries, unthawed
¾ cup unrefined cane sugar, honey, or maple syrup
1 cup water
1 cinnamon stick

1. Place all ingredients in a large saucepan. Bring to a boil and stir until sugar is dissolved. Reduce heat and simmer uncovered until cranberries burst, about 10 minutes. Remove from heat. Cool completely at room temperature and then chill in refrigerator. Cranberry sauce will thicken as it cools.

2. Store in an airtight container in the refrigerator for 3 days or in the freezer for up to 6 months.

Jellied Cranberry Sauce

Love cranberry sauce with your turkey at Thanksgiving? Try this tantalizing cranberry jelly at your next feast, and I bet you'll love it even more than the one that comes out of a can.

HANDS-ON: 20 minutes

INACTIVE: 12 hours

READY IN: 12 hours

DIFFICULTY LEVEL: ★ ★ ★

YIELD: Serves 6; Makes 3 cups

COST PER SERVING: $ $ $

GF DF EF

CALORIES: 91

FAT: 0 g

PROTEIN: 2 g

SODIUM: 10 mg

FIBER: 5 g

CARBOHYDRATES: 15 g

SUGAR: 5 g

24 ounces fresh or frozen cranberries, unthawed

1½ cups honey

1 cup dry white wine

1¼ cups water

½ cup pure cranberry juice or cold water

2 tablespoons unflavored gelatin

1.   Place cranberries, honey, wine, and water in a large saucepan and bring to a boil. Stir; then reduce heat to medium-low and simmer uncovered, stirring occasionally, until the berries have burst, 7–8 minutes.

2.   Place a colander over a large bowl and line with cheesecloth. Pour the cranberry mixture into the colander and let sit until all the juices have drained, about 15 minutes. Compost the solids.

3.   Measure the liquid in the bowl—you should have about 2 cups. Either reduce the liquid by simmering or add water if the liquid is inadequate. Chill if liquid is not cold.

4.   Pour the cold cranberry juice into a small saucepan and sprinkle the gelatin over. Let stand 3–4 minutes to soften. Then, over very low heat, warm the mixture just until the gelatin is dissolved. Pour the gelatin mixture into the cranberry liquid, stir, and then pour into a mold or small bowl. Skim off any bubbles or foam. Cool to room temperature; then cover and refrigerate for at least 12 hours until fully set.

5.   To serve, unmold cranberry sauce and place on a plate. To store, cover mold or plate with plastic wrap and set in the refrigerator for up to 3 days.

Classic Salsa

HANDS-ON: 10 minutes

INACTIVE: none

READY IN: 10 minutes

DIFFICULTY LEVEL: ★

YIELD: Serves 8; Makes 2 cups

COST PER SERVING: $ $

CALORIES: 18

FAT: 0 g

PROTEIN: 1 g

SODIUM: 3 mg

FIBER: 1 g

CARBOHYDRATES: 4 g

SUGAR: 2 g

This recipe is about as easy as they come, as it's fresh, delicious, and easy to customize to your own tastes. It's perfect on tortilla chips, spooned over roasted chicken, or cooked inside your favorite enchiladas.

1 pound tomatoes (about 5–6 Roma-size tomatoes), peeled, seeded, and finely chopped

1 small yellow onion, finely chopped

1–2 jalapeño peppers, seeded and finely minced

3 cloves garlic, finely chopped

½ bunch cilantro, finely chopped

Juice of ½ a lime

1. Toss all ingredients together in a large bowl. To serve fresh, toss in one generous pinch of sea salt and let sit for at least 1 hour to allow flavors to mingle.

2. Store in the refrigerator for up to 3 days.

Pico de Gallo

HANDS-ON: 10 minutes

INACTIVE: 20–30 minutes

READY IN: 30 minutes

DIFFICULTY LEVEL: ★

YIELD: Serves 16; Makes 4 cups

COST PER SERVING: $ $

CALORIES: 13

FAT: 0 g

PROTEIN: 1 g

SODIUM: 77 mg

FIBER: 1 g

CARBOHYDRATES: 3 g

SUGAR: 2 g

Pico de gallo is a traditional Mexican salsa that is reminiscent of the Classic Salsa listed. Pico de gallo is traditionally left a bit chunkier, which makes it all the easier for scooping. And with two types of chili peppers, it's fresh and zingy!

2 pounds tomatoes (10–12 Roma-size tomatoes), seeded and chopped

1 small yellow onion, diced

5–6 stems fresh cilantro, chopped

1 jalapeño pepper, seeded and diced

1 serrano chili, seeded and diced (optional)

2 cloves garlic, minced

Juice of ½ a lime

1 generous pinch of sea salt

Freshly ground black pepper, to taste

1. Toss all ingredients together in a large bowl. Let sit for 20–30 minutes to allow flavors to mingle.

2. Store in the refrigerator for up to 3 days.

Salsa Verde

Tomatillos are cute little vegetables that look like a green tomato covered in a papery husk. Don't miss this chance to get to know them!

HANDS-ON: 25 minutes

INACTIVE: none

READY IN: 25 minutes

DIFFICULTY LEVEL: ★ ★

YIELD: Serves 16; Makes 1 quart

COST PER SERVING: $ $

GF

CALORIES: 23

FAT: 1 g

PROTEIN: 1 g

SODIUM: 149 mg

FIBER: 1 g

CARBOHYDRATES: 3 g

SUGAR: 2 g

12–15 tomatillos

8 cloves garlic, peeled and left whole

1–2 jalapeños, coarsely chopped

2 poblano, serrano, or Anaheim peppers

½ bunch cilantro

1 white or yellow onion, coarsely chopped

1 teaspoon salt

1 tablespoon olive oil or lard

1 tablespoon lime juice

1. Place the whole tomatillos and garlic cloves in a stockpot and cover with water. Bring to a boil over medium-high heat; then reduce the heat to medium and simmer uncovered until the tomatillos are soft and no longer bright green, about 10 minutes.

2. Place the tomatillos, garlic, and about ½ cup of the cooking liquid in a blender. Purée; then add the jalapeños, poblanos, cilantro, onion, and salt, and purée again until smooth.

3. Heat the oil or lard in the same stockpot over medium-high heat. Once it is hot but not smoking, pour in the salsa and bring to a simmer. Let it simmer uncovered over medium heat until it thickens and deepens in color, 5–7 minutes. Remove from the heat, stir in the lime juice, and add more salt, if needed. Cool completely.

4. To store, place in an airtight container and place in the refrigerator for up to 1 week.

Cherry Chutney

This chutney rivals any you would find in any store and goes especially well with pork, duck, chicken, and salmon. If you have access to lots of cherries during cherry season, it works well to make a large batch and freeze in smaller portions to use whenever you want a reminder of summer in the middle of the dark, dreary winter.

HANDS-ON: 20 minutes

INACTIVE: 1½ hours

READY IN: 2 hours

DIFFICULTY LEVEL: ★ ★

YIELD: Serves 6; Makes 3 cups

COST PER SERVING: $ $

CALORIES: 149

FAT: 0 g

PROTEIN: 1 g

SODIUM: 397 mg

FIBER: 2 g

CARBOHYDRATES: 35 g

SUGAR: 30 g

1 pound cherries, pitted

1 cup cider vinegar

½ cup rice vinegar

1 large onion, chopped

1 apple, peeled, cored, and chopped

½ cup unrefined cane sugar

2 tablespoons minced fresh ginger

2 tablespoons Chinese five-spice powder

1 teaspoon salt

¼ teaspoon ground nutmeg

1. Place all ingredients into a large pot. Bring to a simmer over medium-high heat; then reduce heat to medium-low, cover, and simmer for 1 hour, stirring occasionally. Remove the lid, and continue simmering for another 15–20 minutes. Chill before serving.

2. To store, place in an airtight container and set in the refrigerator for up to 5 days or in the freezer for up to 3 months.

Apricot Preserves

This is an old French recipe and it embodies the best of French country cooking—simple and flavorful. By keeping the pits in the recipe, the flavor of the apricots is deepened and just a touch of almond is imparted.

HANDS-ON: 20 minutes

INACTIVE: 45 minutes

READY IN: 1 hour

DIFFICULTY LEVEL: ★ ★ ★

YIELD: Serves 24; Makes 6 cups

COST PER SERVING: $ $

GF V DF EF

CALORIES: 113

FAT: 0 g

PROTEIN: 1 g

SODIUM: 2 mg

FIBER: 1 g

CARBOHYDRATES: 30 g

SUGAR: 28 g

3 pounds apricots

1 cup water

2 cups honey

Juice of 1 lemon

¼ cup almonds (optional)

1. Wash the apricots; then cut them open and remove the pits, but do not discard them.

2. Coarsely chop the apricots and set them aside.

3. Crack open one pit by laying the long side of a large knife against it and smashing it with your hand. Take out the almond-like nut inside and bite it—if it's sweet, crack all the remaining pits and forego the use of the additional, optional almonds, but if it's bitter, crack just three of the pits and use regular almonds. Coarsely chop the nuts and wrap in one thin layer of cheesecloth.

4. In a large, heavy-bottomed saucepan, bring the water and honey to a full, rolling boil over medium-high heat. Add in the apricots, lemon juice, and nuts and continue to cook uncovered at a heavy simmer until the apricots are very soft and the mixture is syrupy, about 30 minutes. Stir occasionally to be sure the mixture isn't sticking to the bottom and skim off any foam that forms on the top.

5. You can test the doneness of the preserves by spooning a bit of the syrup onto a cold plate. If it gels, it's done.

6. Remove from the heat and spoon into jars. Store in the refrigerator for up to 3 months.

Grape Jelly

Homemade grape jelly is one of those little satisfactions that brings a smile to your face every time you stumble upon one of the jars in your pantry. The thing with jelly is that the sugar is included in order to help the jelly set properly, not just to sweeten it, so traditional jams and jellies—this one included—call for very large amounts of sugar. If you are wanting or needing to use less sugar or would like to use alternative forms of sugar, such as honey or stevia, find a brand of low-sugar pectin, such as Pomona's Universal Pectin or Ball RealFruit No-Sugar Pectin, and follow the directions on the box instead of the directions here. Low-sugar pectins are sometimes difficult to find locally, but you can find them fairly easily from multiple sources online.

HANDS ON: 30 minutes

INACTIVE: none

READY IN: 30 minutes

DIFFICULTY LEVEL: ★ ★

YIELD: Serves 16; Makes 4 pints

COST PER SERVING: $ $

CALORIES: 210

FAT: 0 g

PROTEIN: 0 g

SODIUM: 9 mg

FIBER: 0 g

CARBOHYDRATES: 51 g

SUGAR: 51 g

3 cups grape juice

4 tablespoons powdered pectin

3½ cups sugar

1. Place grape juice in an large saucepan. Gradually stir in pectin and whisk to make sure there are no lumps. Place on high heat and bring mixture to a full, rolling boil that cannot be stirred down, stirring constantly.

2. Once you've established a hard boil, add the sugar, stirring to dissolve. Return mixture to a full boil. Boil hard for 1 minute, stirring constantly. Remove from heat. Skim foam if desired.

3. Ladle the jelly into clean jars.

4. To store the jelly for up to 1 year, process the hot jars of jelly for 10 minutes in a boiling water bath.

5. To enjoy more immediately, let the jelly cool to room temperature; then store in the refrigerator for up to 3 weeks.

Fig Newton Butter

This fruit butter starts with dehydrated fruit rather than fresh fruit. This technique is advantageous for a number of reasons. First, dehydrating concentrates the sugars, so less sweetener is needed when making the fruit butter. Second, in the summertime when all your fruit is ripening at once, it allows you to preserve the harvest quickly and efficiently using a food dehydrator and then make other products, such as this fruit butter, later on. Lastly, this fruit butter is absolutely kid-friendly, even a kid-favorite, making it an excellent way to introduce or increase the amount of probiotics in your child's diet. Feel free to substitute other dried fruits as well—fig and apple just happen to be favorites of mine. Try Cinnamon Raisin by substituting raisins for the figs and apples; then spread the finished butter on sourdough toast for a quick and dirty version of cinnamon swirl toast. Or try Peach Butter using peaches and lemon zest. The options are endless!

HANDS ON: 10 minutes

INACTIVE: 20 minutes

READY IN: 30 minutes

DIFFICULTY LEVEL: ★

YIELD: Serves 6; Makes 1½ cups

COST PER SERVING: $ $

GF

CALORIES: 63

FAT: 0 g

PROTEIN: 1 g

SODIUM: 201 mg

FIBER: 3 g

CARBOHYDRATES: 16 g

SUGAR: 12 g

¾ **cup dried figs**

¼ **cup dried apples**

1½–2 **cups warm filtered water**

Zest of 1 small orange

½ **teaspoon salt**

1–2 **tablespoons honey (optional)**

½ **teaspoon cinnamon (optional)**

1. Coarsely chop the figs and apples and place in a bowl. Cover with warm filtered water and let sit for 20–25 minutes until softened. Drain well, reserving the soaking water.

2. Place the softened fruit in a food processor with the orange zest and salt. Process until a smooth paste forms, adding a teaspoon or so of the reserved water if necessary. Stir in the honey and cinnamon, if desired.

3. Store in an airtight container in the refrigerator for up to 1 week.

Berry Jam

You can use any berries you'd like for this jam—it's a very versatile recipe. The apple is included merely because it has naturally occurring pectin and helps the jam gel, but most berries will gel just fine even without the apple.

HANDS-ON: 5 minutes

INACTIVE: 20–30 minutes

READY IN: 30 minutes

DIFFICULTY LEVEL: ★

YIELD: Serves 24; Makes 1½ cups

COST PER SERVING: $

CALORIES: 146

FAT: 0 g

PROTEIN: 0 g

SODIUM: 1 mg

FIBER: 1 g

CARBOHYDRATES: 38 g

SUGAR: 36 g

4 cups crushed berries

4 cups sugar

2 tablespoons lemon juice

½ tart apple, peeled, cored, and diced finely (optional)

1. Combine the berries, sugar, lemon juice, and apple, if using, in a large saucepan and turn the heat to high. Bring to a boil and let it boil rapidly for 5 minutes. Reduce to medium heat and cook uncovered an additional 15 minutes.

2. After 15 minutes, put a drop of the jam on a cold plate and let it sit for a few moments. Push the edge of the drop with your finger and watch to see if it wrinkles. If it does, the jam is done.

3. Skim off any foam, cool, and store in an airtight container in the refrigerator for up to 3 weeks. Remember that the jam will thicken as it cools.

Crunchy Garlic-Dill Pickles (Lacto-Fermented)

These delicious pickles are always worth the wait! While they take 5–8 days to make, the end result is unlike anything you've ever had before. Chances are, you'll chow through a jar of these in one sitting, so you may want make several jars at once, just so you're never out.

HANDS ON: 15 minutes

INACTIVE: 5–8 days

READY IN: 8 days

DIFFICULTY LEVEL: ★

YIELD: Serves 8; Makes 1 quart

COST PER SERVING: $

CALORIES: 11

FAT: 0 g

PROTEIN: 0.5 g

SODIUM: 425 mg

FIBER: 0.5 g

CARBOHYDRATES: 2.5 g

SUGAR: 1 g

1 pound small pickling cucumbers
1 large horseradish leaf or grape leaf, or 1 tablespoon loose-leaf black tea
2 large dill tops with flower or seed head
4–6 whole garlic cloves
2 tablespoons unrefined sea salt
1–1½ cups filtered water, to cover

1. First, prepare your cucumbers by washing them well.

2. Pack the horseradish leaf, cucumbers, dill, and garlic cloves tightly into a quart-size Mason jar, leaving about 1" of headspace at the top of the jar.

3. Stir the salt into the water until it's dissolved.

4. Pour the salt solution into the jar, adding more fresh water if necessary to completely cover the cucumbers by at least half an inch. Cover loosely with a towel and secure with a rubber band; then set aside at room temperature for 5–8 days.

5. Check the top of the jar each day through the glass and remove the towel only if you need to attend to the ferment—if you see any mold, just scrape it off. Top off with water if there is less than half an inch above the pickles.

6. Anytime in the 5- to 8-day period, replace the towel with the jar's proper lid and move it to the refrigerator for long-term storage. Pickles will last up for 6 months in the refrigerator.

Bread and Butter Pickles

Bread and butter pickles are one of those foods that seems to show up on every buffet and holiday table. The lacto-fermented method of making pickles is great because it turns out perfect pickles almost every time and requires very little hands-on time at the beginning, compared to other methods.

HANDS ON: 10 minutes

INACTIVE: 5–8 days

READY IN: 8 days

DIFFICULTY LEVEL: ★

YIELD: Serves 8; Makes 1 quart

COST PER SERVING: $ $

CALORIES: 12

FAT: 0 g

PROTEIN: 0.5 g

SODIUM: 365 mg

FIBER: 0.5 g

CARBOHYDRATES: 2.5 g

SUGAR: 1 g

1 pound small pickling cucumbers, sliced into ¼" coins

2 tablespoons pickling spice

1 tablespoon black peppercorns

2–3 garlic cloves

2–3 dill fronds

2 tablespoons unrefined sea salt

1–1½ cups fresh water, to cover

1. First, prepare your cucumbers by washing them well.

2. Pour the pickling spice and peppercorns into the bottom of a quart-size Mason jar. Pack the cucumbers, garlic cloves, and dill fronds tightly in, leaving at least 1½" of headspace at the top of the jar.

3. Stir the salt into the water until it's dissolved, then pour the salt solution into the jar, adding more fresh water if necessary to completely cover the cucumbers by at least half an inch. Cover loosely; then set aside at room temperature for 5–8 days.

4. Check the top of the jar each day through the glass and remove the cover only if you need to attend to the ferment—if you see any mold, just scrape it off. Top off with water if there is less than half an inch above the pickles.

5. Anytime in the 5- to 8-day period, replace the towel with the jar's proper lid and move it to the refrigerator for long-term storage. Pickles will last up for 6 months in the refrigerator.

Tahini

The toasted sesame and the creamy texture of tahini are perfect for a wide range of recipes, and thus, it is a must-have staple in any pantry. Use this yummy spread to make hummus, baba ghanouj, and other dips and spreads.

HANDS-ON: 15 minutes

INACTIVE: none

READY IN: 15 minutes

DIFFICULTY LEVEL: ★

YIELD: Serves 16; Makes 4 cups

COST PER SERVING: $ $

GF V DF EF

CALORIES: 280

FAT: 26 g

PROTEIN: 6 g

SODIUM: 4 mg

FIBER: 4 g

CARBOHYDRATES: 8 g

SUGAR: 0 g

4 cups sesame seeds
½ cup olive oil
1–2 tablespoons toasted sesame oil

1. Preheat a large, dry sauté pan over medium heat and pour in the sesame seeds. Toss or stir the seeds every 15–20 seconds until they are toasted and fragrant, 4–6 minutes.

2. Pour the sesame seeds into a food processor and blend until the seeds are powdered and beginning to turn into sesame butter. Slowly drizzle in the olive oil. Blend for 4–8 minutes until the mixture is thick and smooth. Add the toasted sesame oil and more olive oil, if needed, and blend once again until smooth.

3. Store the tahini in an airtight container for about 3 months at room temperature.

CHAPTER 8

Salad Dressings, Spices, and Seasonings

Like a good sauce, good spices can elevate a dish from good to amazing. Just imagine a pot of chili without chili powder, a pasta sauce without oregano, or a Jamaican jerk rub without allspice. There's just something missing. This chapter focuses on how to make your own spice blends, whip up a salad dressing, and make your own taco seasoning. When you have access to fresh herbs from your garden, you can dry them by using a food dehydrator for a couple of hours or placing the herbs in the oven at the lowest temperature for 10 hours. Not only is this cost-effective; it allows you to personalize your spice blends according to taste. Dried herbs can be stored for 6–12 months, so you'll always have them on hand to perk up any meal or dressing!

Caesar Dressing

HANDS-ON: 10 minutes

INACTIVE: none

READY IN: 10 minutes

DIFFICULTY LEVEL: ★ ★

YIELD: Serves 8; Makes 1 cup

COST PER SERVING: $

CALORIES: 225

FAT: 18 g

PROTEIN: 12 g

SODIUM: 68 mg

FIBER: 0 g

CARBOHYDRATES: 1 g

SUGAR: 0 g

This dressing is typically served on crispy romaine lettuce with copious amounts of freshly ground black pepper and salty Parmesan cheese. It is also fantastic slathered on hefty whole grain bread or, when the weather is cold, as an accompaniment to a hearty soup.

2 egg yolks

3 cloves garlic, minced finely

1 tablespoon lemon juice

1 tablespoon Dijon-style mustard

5 or 6 anchovy fillets, or 1 tablespoon anchovy paste

2 teaspoons red wine vinegar

1 teaspoon Worcestershire sauce

¼ teaspoon black pepper

½ cup extra-virgin olive oil

1. Combine all ingredients, except for the oil, in a food processor and process until thoroughly mixed. Then, with the motor running, drizzle in the olive oil as slowly as possible. The mixture will thicken noticeably.

2. Store in the refrigerator for up to 1 week.

Ranch Dressing

HANDS-ON: 5 minutes

INACTIVE: none

READY IN: 5 minutes

DIFFICULTY LEVEL: ★

YIELD: Serves 6; Makes 1½ cups

COST PER SERVING: $ $

CALORIES: 284

FAT: 31 g

PROTEIN: 1 g

SODIUM: 413 mg

FIBER: 0 g

CARBOHYDRATES: 1.5 g

SUGAR: 0.5 g

This popular salad dressing and dip features fresh herbs, which make it heavenly. It's a crowd-pleaser, whether you're serving it to toddlers at lunch or next to a crudités platter at an all-adult party.

1 cup mayonnaise

2 cloves garlic, minced

¼ cup cultured buttermilk or sour cream

¼ cup (combined) minced fresh herbs (basil, parsley, dill, and chives)

¼ teaspoon freshly ground black pepper

½ teaspoon salt

1. Combine all ingredients in a medium bowl and whisk well. Serve immediately or set in the refrigerator for at least 30 minutes to allow flavors to meld.

2. Keeps well in the refrigerator for up to 5 days.

Dry Ranch Dressing Mix

HANDS-ON: 5 minutes

INACTIVE: none

READY IN: 5 minutes

DIFFICULTY LEVEL: ★

YIELD: Serves 16; Makes 1 cup

COST PER SERVING: $

CALORIES: 284

FAT: 31 g

PROTEIN: 1 g

SODIUM: 413 mg

FIBER: 0 g

CARBOHYDRATES: 1.5 g

SUGAR: 0.5 g

This recipe is your whole food answer to the little packets of dry ranch powder that are so easy to mix up but that contain more artificial ingredients than natural ones. Use it for ranch dip, ranch dressing, or your favorite party chip dip.

½ cup dried parsley	**2 tablespoons onion powder**
2 tablespoons dried dill	**2 teaspoons salt**
2 tablespoons garlic powder	**Pinch of black pepper**

1. Mix ingredients well and store in a sealed container for 6–12 months.

2. Mix 1 tablespoon of the mix with ½ cup mayonnaise and ¼ cup sour cream for ranch dip.

3. Mix 1 tablespoon of the mix with ½ cup mayonnaise and ⅓ cup buttermilk for ranch dressing.

4. Adjust to taste. Shake well before serving. Once mixed, store in the refrigerator in an airtight container for up to 1 week.

Blue Cheese Dressing

HANDS-ON: 5 minutes

INACTIVE: 8 hours

READY IN: 8 hours

DIFFICULTY LEVEL: ★

YIELD: Serves 8; Makes 2 cups

COST PER SERVING: $ $

CALORIES: 9

FAT: 0 g

PROTEIN: 0.5 g

SODIUM: 299 mg

FIBER: 0.5 g

CARBOHYDRATES: 2 g

SUGAR: 0 g

If you've got the time, let this dressing chill overnight—the flavors will develop excellently.

½ cup mayonnaise
¼ cup well-shaken cultured buttermilk
2 tablespoons sour cream, piima cream, or soured raw cream
3 tablespoons extra-virgin olive oil
2 tablespoons red wine vinegar
1 tablespoon raw honey or maple syrup
2 large cloves garlic, finely grated
Small pinch of freshly ground black pepper
¾ cup crumbled blue cheese

1. Whisk all ingredients together, adding blue cheese only after the rest of the dressing is smooth. Let sit for at least 8 hours before serving for the best flavor.

2. Store in the refrigerator in an airtight container for up to 1 week.

Creamy Lemon-Avocado Dressing

This is an amazingly yummy dressing—perky and fresh from the lemon and creamy from the avocado. For the smoothest texture, use a blender or a food processor, but you may certainly mash and whisk by hand as well. The flavor will still come through even though the texture is a bit chunkier.

HANDS-ON: 10 minutes

INACTIVE: 5 minutes

READY IN: 15 minutes

DIFFICULTY LEVEL: ★

YIELD: Serves 4; Makes 1 cup

COST PER SERVING: $ $

GF V DF EF

CALORIES: 212

FAT: 21 g

PROTEIN: 1 g

SODIUM: 299 mg

FIBER: 2.5 g

CARBOHYDRATES: 5 g

SUGAR: 2 g

1 tablespoon fennel seeds

3 scallions, coarsely chopped

Juice of ½ a lemon

½ avocado, perfectly ripe

⅓ cup extra-virgin olive oil or avocado oil

1 teaspoon raw honey or evaporated cane sugar

½ teaspoon sea salt, or to taste

Freshly ground pepper, to taste

1.   First, soften the fennel seeds by placing them in a small bowl with hot water for 5 minutes. Drain well.

2.   Place the scallions, fennel seeds, lemon juice, and avocado in a food processor and pulse until well chopped. Slowly drizzle in the oil; then add the honey, salt, and pepper. Adjust seasonings to taste.

3.   Store in the refrigerator in an airtight container for up to 2 days.

Italian Dressing

This Italian dressing has all the flavor of your favorite bottled brands, but uses healthy oils and features a number of herbs to fill out the flavor rather than artificial flavor enhancers. If your favorite store-bought brand contains Parmesan cheese and you find yourself missing it, by all means, feel free to toss in a quarter-cup as you whisk.

HANDS-ON: 10 minutes

INACTIVE: none

READY IN: 10 minutes

DIFFICULTY LEVEL: ★

YIELD: Serves 10; Makes 1¼ cups

COST PER SERVING: $

GF V DF EF

CALORIES: 101

FAT: 10 g

PROTEIN: 0.5 g

SODIUM: 140 mg

FIBER: 0 g

CARBOHYDRATES: 1 g

SUGAR: 0.5 g

½ cup olive oil

6 tablespoons white wine vinegar

2 tablespoons chopped fresh parsley

1 tablespoon fresh lemon juice

2–3 garlic cloves, chopped

2–3 fresh basil leaves, minced, or 1 teaspoon dried basil (optional)

2–3 tablespoons chopped fresh oregano, or 2 teaspoons dried oregano

¼ teaspoon dried crushed red pepper

½ teaspoon unrefined sea salt

4–5 sun-dried tomatoes, finely chopped

1. Finely chop all ingredients, combine in a small bowl, and whisk to blend.

2. Alternatively, for a creamier dressing, place all ingredients except for olive oil in a food processor and pulse to combine. Then, with the motor running, drizzle in the olive oil, which will create a thick, egg-free, Caesar-style dressing.

3. Store in the refrigerator in an airtight container for up to 2 weeks.

Thousand Island Dressing

Thousand Island dressing is delicious on iceberg lettuce any time of year, but my favorite use for it is at St. Patrick's Day for making Reuben sandwiches—toasted sourdough bread slathered with Thousand Island, then layered high with cured corned beef, Swiss cheese, and sauerkraut. It's a fitting all-American sandwich for a spirited Irish-American holiday. Slàinte!

HANDS-ON: 10 minutes

INACTIVE: none

READY IN: 10 minutes

DIFFICULTY LEVEL: ★

YIELD: Serves 14; Makes 1¾ cups

COST PER SERVING: $ $

GF   DF

CALORIES: 160

FAT: 16 g

PROTEIN: 1 g

SODIUM: 314 mg

FIBER: 0 g

CARBOHYDRATES: 3 g

SUGAR: 2.4 g

1 whole egg

2 egg yolks

1 teaspoon Dijon mustard

1½ tablespoons lemon juice

Generous pinch of salt

1 cup extra-virgin olive oil or sunflower oil

¼ cup ketchup

2 tablespoons apple cider vinegar

½ teaspoon smoked paprika

2 tablespoons prepared horseradish

Generous dash of Worcestershire sauce

1 tablespoon unrefined cane sugar or honey

1 tablespoon minced parsley

½ teaspoon sea salt

2 teaspoons chopped pickles (dill or sweet, your choice)

1 tablespoon minced onion

1. In the bowl of a food processor, combine the eggs, mustard, lemon juice, and salt. Keep the blades running to combine thoroughly.

2. Pour in the oil extremely slowly. Start with mere drops; then work up to pouring it in a thin stream. You'll notice when the oil is fully emulsified, as the sound will change.

3. When the mayonnaise is finished, add in all remaining ingredients. Pulse several times to combine thoroughly.

4. Store in the refrigerator for up to 1 week.

Green Goddess Dressing

Green goddess dressing reigned in American kitchens for several decades before ranch dressing gained popularity through the 1960s. In this version, you'll add spinach to the mix to give it an extra green kick. If you want to heighten the green color of the dressing even more, juice a few stems of parsley and pour in the fresh parsley juice.

HANDS ON: 10 minutes

INACTIVE: none

READY IN: 10 minutes

DIFFICULTY LEVEL: ★

YIELD: Serves 12; Makes 1½ cups

COST PER SERVING: $ $

CALORIES: 142

FAT: 12 g

PROTEIN: 7 g

SODIUM: 139 mg

FIBER: 0.5 g

CARBOHYDRATES: 1 g

SUGAR: 0 g

2 egg yolks

3 cloves garlic, coarsely chopped

1 shallot, minced

1 tablespoon lemon juice

1 teaspoon Dijon-style mustard

5–6 anchovy fillets, or 1 tablespoon anchovy paste

2 teaspoons white wine vinegar

5–6 ounces spinach leaves, chopped

¼ cup chopped fresh parsley

1 teaspoon chopped fresh tarragon

2 tablespoons chopped fresh chives

½ teaspoon sea salt

¼ teaspoon black pepper

½ cup extra-virgin olive oil

1. Combine all ingredients, except for the oil, in a food processor and process until the greens are very thoroughly minced.

2. Then, with the motor running, drizzle in the olive oil as slowly as possible. Start with mere drops; then work up to pouring it in a thin stream. When all the oil is added, the dressing should be thick. If it's not, add an additional 1–2 tablespoons of oil.

3. Store in the refrigerator for up to 1 week.

Asian Sesame Dressing

If you love Asian flavors, this dressing is for you. The toasted sesame oil provides that enticing nutty flavor that only sesame can provide, the apple cider vinegar acts as a digestive aid, and the raw soy sauce provides a healthy wallop of live enzymes. To top it off, the raw garlic and ginger will boost your system's immunity, so this dressing will not only accompany your next salad beautifully, but will make your whole body happy, too.

HANDS-ON: 5 minutes

INACTIVE: none

READY IN: 5 minutes

DIFFICULTY LEVEL: ★

YIELD: Serves 10; Makes 1¼ cups

COST PER SERVING: $

CALORIES: 142

FAT: 15 g

PROTEIN: 0.5 g

SODIUM: 360 mg

FIBER: 0 g

CARBOHYDRATES: 1 g

SUGAR: 0 g

½ cup extra-virgin olive oil

3 tablespoons toasted sesame oil

3 tablespoons apple cider vinegar

¼ cup raw soy sauce

1 tablespoon white or black sesame seeds, toasted

2 cloves garlic, finely minced

2 teaspoons finely minced fresh ginger

1. Place all ingredients in a medium bowl and whisk to combine.

2. Store in the refrigerator in an airtight container for up to 1 week.

Baba Ghanouj

Traditionally, baba ghanouj is served slightly chunky, but this recipe produces a much smoother spread. Process the eggplant to your preferred consistency.

HANDS-ON: 15 minutes

INACTIVE: 45 minutes

READY IN: 1 hour

DIFFICULTY LEVEL: ★ ★

YIELD: Serves 6; Makes 3 cups

COST PER SERVING: $ $

CALORIES: 112

FAT: 7 g

PROTEIN: 3 g

SODIUM: 206 mg

FIBER: 6 g

CARBOHYDRATES: 11 g

SUGAR: 3 g

2 pounds eggplant (any variety)

2 tablespoons extra-virgin olive oil, plus more as needed

2 tablespoons tahini

3 garlic cloves, coarsely chopped

1 teaspoon ground cumin

Juice of 1 lemon, divided

½ teaspoon sea salt (or more, to taste)

1 generous pinch smoked paprika (or more, to taste)

2 tablespoons water, plus more as needed

1 tablespoon chopped parsley

1. Preheat the oven to 400°F. Poke the eggplants in several places with the tines of a fork or a paring knife; then cut them in half lengthwise and brush them lightly with olive oil. Place on a parchment paper–lined baking sheet, cut-side down, and roast until very tender, 25–40 minutes (depending on the variety and thickness of the eggplant). Remove from oven and set aside until they're cool enough to handle.

2. Scoop the eggplant flesh into the bowl of a food processor or a mortar and pestle. Add the olive oil, tahini, garlic, cumin, half of the lemon juice, salt, paprika, and 2 tablespoons water. Pulse until fully combined; then either remove to a bowl if you like a chunky texture or continue to process for a smooth paste. Add more olive oil or water as needed.

3. Allow the baba ghanouj to cool to room temperature; then taste and adjust seasonings with the remaining lemon juice, salt, and paprika. To serve, drizzle olive oil on the top and sprinkle with parsley.

4. Store in the refrigerator in an airtight container for up to 5 days.

Hummus

Hummus is great for satisfying afternoon cravings. This plain, original version is absolutely delicious, but there are a few add-ins that are worth adding in as well—roasted garlic, kalamata olives, or roasted red peppers.

HANDS-ON: 10 minutes

INACTIVE: none

READY IN: 10 minutes

DIFFICULTY LEVEL: ★

YIELD: Serves 6; Makes 3½ cups

COST PER SERVING: $ $

GF V V DF EF

CALORIES: 121

FAT: 4 g

PROTEIN: 6 g

SODIUM: 402 mg

FIBER: 4.5 g

CARBOHYDRATES: 16 g

SUGAR: 2.5 g

2 cups cooked garbanzo beans

3 cloves garlic, coarsely chopped

2 tablespoons tahini

Juice of ½ a lemon

1 generous pinch sea salt

2 tablespoons water, plus more if needed

1. Pulse beans and garlic in a food processor until roughly blended; then add in the remaining ingredients and process until smooth. Add more water as necessary to obtain your preferred consistency.

2. Store in the refrigerator in an airtight container for up to 5 days.

Creamy Spinach-Artichoke Dip

What party or gathering is complete without a creamy spinach-artichoke dip? If you use additive-free cream cheese, sour cream, and mayonnaise, such as the ones found in Chapters 5 and 6 of this book, or by purchasing local, conscientiously made products that don't use carrageenan, gums, or other artificial thickeners, this dip is a nourishing treat that is sure to please.

HANDS-ON: 10 minutes

INACTIVE: 20 minutes–3 hours

READY IN: 3 hours

DIFFICULTY LEVEL: ★

YIELD: Serves 10; Makes 5 cups

COST PER SERVING: $ $

GF

CALORIES: 146

FAT: 13 g

PROTEIN: 5 g

SODIUM: 406 mg

FIBER: 2 g

CARBOHYDRATES: 5 g

SUGAR: 1 g

¼ cup sour cream

8 ounces cream cheese

¼ cup mayonnaise

1 pound blanched, chopped spinach leaves, well drained

4 cloves garlic, minced

⅓ cup finely grated Parmesan cheese

2 shallots, finely chopped

1½ cups diced artichoke hearts

Few drops of fresh lemon juice

¼ teaspoon smoked paprika (optional)

1 pinch unrefined sea salt

Freshly ground black pepper, to taste

1. Mix together the sour cream, cream cheese, and mayonnaise. Combine with the other ingredients and mix well. If serving cold, cover and refrigerate for several hours to allow the flavors to meld. If a warm dip is preferred, place in an ovensafe dish and bake at 350°F for 20 minutes.

2. Store in the refrigerator for up to 2 days, although the texture will be best immediately.

Chili Powder

The delightful thing about making your own chili powder is that you are completely in control of flavor. Although, that can be a bit tricky since many of us are quite ignorant about the flavor nuances of different chilies. Just like it takes a sommelier to help you choose just the right wine, find a Latin market with helpful staff—or even better, dried chilies in bulk bins where you can stick your nose in and discover your favorites. Common favorites are anchos, chiles de árbol, guajillos, and chipotles. Also, you may wonder why there are other spices in this recipe since it is "chili powder," not "chili and other spices powder." Basically, while you can absolutely make chili powder using just dried chilies, often that creates a chili powder with an explosive chili blast, which is wonderful for chili but a bit overwhelming in an enchilada sauce or other more nuanced dishes. Thus, for everyday use, I prefer a chili powder blended with garlic, cumin, oregano, and paprika.

HANDS-ON: 10 minutes

INACTIVE: none

READY IN: 10 minutes

DIFFICULTY LEVEL: ★ ★

YIELD: Serves 16; Makes 1 cup

COST PER SERVING: $

CALORIES: 26

FAT: 0.5 g

PROTEIN: 1.5 g

SODIUM: 6 mg

FIBER: 1 g

CARBOHYDRATES: 5 g

SUGAR: 2 g

3 tablespoons whole cumin seeds

2 cascabel chilies, stemmed, seeded, and sliced

6 chipotle chilies, stemmed, seeded, and sliced

4 guajillo chilies, stemmed, seeded, and sliced

4 tablespoons garlic powder

2 tablespoons dried oregano

2 teaspoons smoked paprika

1. Preheat a small sauté pan over medium-high heat; then add the cumin seeds. Dry-roast, tossing often, until you begin to smell the cumin toasting, 4–5 minutes. Set aside and cool completely. (If any of your chilies are leathery rather than brittle and dry, you can add them as well.)

2. Once cool, place all ingredients in a blender. Process until everything becomes a fine powder. Store in an airtight container for up to 6 months.

Taco Seasoning

HANDS-ON: 5 minutes

INACTIVE: none

READY IN: 5 minutes

DIFFICULTY LEVEL: ★

YIELD: Serves 16; Makes 1 cup

COST PER SERVING: $

CALORIES: 16

FAT: 0.5 g

PROTEIN: 1 g

SODIUM: 469 mg

FIBER: 1.5 g

CARBOHYDRATES: 3 g

SUGAR: 0.5 g

You might be able to make tacos without lettuce or tomatoes on hand, but you can't make tacos without taco seasoning. Unlike some store-bought versions, this taco seasoning features spices and nothing more—no preservatives, no anticaking agents, no hydrogenated oils—so mix up a batch to keep at the ready!

⅓ cup chili powder

1 tablespoon garlic powder

1½ teaspoons onion powder

1½ teaspoons crushed red pepper flakes

1 tablespoon dried oregano

1 tablespoon smoked paprika

3 tablespoons ground cumin

1 tablespoon sea salt

1 teaspoon black pepper

Mix together all ingredients; then store in an airtight container for up to 6 months.

Cajun Spice Mix

HANDS-ON: 5 minutes

INACTIVE: none

READY IN: 5 minutes

DIFFICULTY LEVEL: ★

YIELD: Serves 16; Makes 1 cup

COST PER SERVING: $

CALORIES: 18

FAT: 0.5 g

PROTEIN: 1 g

SODIUM: 3.8 mg

FIBER: 1.5 g

CARBOHYDRATES: 4 g

SUGAR: 0.5 g

When you need a spicy kick, Cajun is the way to go, as it gives you a wonderful wallop as well as some really great flavor to go with it.

2 tablespoons onion powder

2 tablespoons garlic powder

2 tablespoons dried oregano

2 tablespoons dried sweet basil

2 tablespoons dried parsley

1 tablespoon dried thyme

1 tablespoon black pepper

1 teaspoon cayenne pepper

1 tablespoon celery seed

5 tablespoons sweet paprika

Combine in a small bowl; then store in an airtight container for up to 6 months.

Homemade Italian Seasoning

HANDS-ON: 5 minutes

INACTIVE: none

READY IN: 5 minutes

DIFFICULTY LEVEL: ★

YIELD: Serves 36; Makes 2¼ cups

COST PER SERVING: $

CALORIES: 5

FAT: 0 g

PROTEIN: 0 g

SODIUM: 1 mg

FIBER: 1 g

CARBOHYDRATES: 1 g

SUGAR: 0 g

This is the perfect blend for your pizzas and pastas, as well as sprinkled liberally over chili, stews, and roasted vegetables.

½ **cup oregano**
½ **cup basil**
½ **cup marjoram**
¼ **cup rosemary, cut finely**
¼ **cup thyme**
¼ **cup sage**

Whisk everything together in a small bowl. Store in an airtight container for about 6 months.

Herbes de Provence Blend

HANDS-ON: 5 minutes

INACTIVE: none

READY IN: 5 minutes

DIFFICULTY LEVEL: ★

YIELD: Serves 16; Makes 1 cup

COST PER SERVING: $

CALORIES: 8

FAT: 0 g

PROTEIN: 0 g

SODIUM: 1 mg

FIBER: 1 g

CARBOHYDRATES: 1.5 g

SUGAR: 0 g

Herbes de Provence is the quintessential spice blend for the modern kitchen, as the flavors meld extremely well with a wide variety of dishes, including roasted meats, roasted vegetables, and hearty stews.

2 **tablespoons dried savory**
2 **tablespoons dried rosemary**
2 **tablespoons dried thyme**
2 **tablespoons dried oregano**
2 **tablespoons dried basil**
2 **tablespoons dried marjoram**
1 **tablespoon dried fennel seed**
1 **tablespoon dried lavender**

In a small mixing bowl, combine all the ingredients together. Store in an airtight container for up to 1 year.

5-Spice Blend

HANDS-ON: 10 minutes

INACTIVE: none

READY IN: 10 minutes

DIFFICULTY LEVEL: ★ ★

YIELD: Serves 12; Makes ¾ cup

COST PER SERVING: $

GF V DF EF

CALORIES: 16

FAT: 0.5 g

PROTEIN: 0.5 g

SODIUM: 3 mg

FIBER: 2 g

CARBOHYDRATES: 3 g

SUGAR: 0 g

Five-Spice is a mixture of five spices commonly used in Chinese cuisine, so it certainly accompanies traditional Chinese foods well. However, this blend is also delicious stirred into applesauce or yogurt, sprinkled over mulled wine or apple cider, or added to holiday spice cookies.

9 star anise

3 tablespoons ground cinnamon

3 tablespoons fennel seed

1 teaspoon freshly ground pepper

2 teaspoons ground cloves

1. Place star anise in a spice grinder or coffee grinder and grind to a fine powder.

2. Mix all ingredients together. Store in an airtight container for up to 6 months.

Jamaican Jerk Blend

HANDS-ON: 5 minutes

INACTIVE: none

READY IN: 5 minutes

DIFFICULTY LEVEL: ★

YIELD: Serves 8; Makes ½ cup

COST PER SERVING: $

GF V DF EF

CALORIES: 17

FAT: 0 g

PROTEIN: 0.5 g

SODIUM: 1,699 mg

FIBER: 1 g

CARBOHYDRATES: 4 g

SUGAR: 0 g

Any dry spice blend made outside of Jamaica itself is a far cry from the "true" flavor of Jamaican jerk that can only result from using fresh cinnamon leaves and roasting meat over allspice wood. Nonetheless, this blend will bring calypso to your tongue and just might make you long to dance in warm sea breezes.

¼ cup onion powder

2 tablespoons salt

2 tablespoons thyme

2 teaspoons ground allspice

1 tablespoon cinnamon

1 teaspoon cayenne powder (optional)

Whisk all ingredients together in a small bowl; then store in an airtight container for up to 6 months.

Thanksgiving Sage Blend

HANDS-ON: 5 minutes

INACTIVE: none

READY IN: 5 minutes

DIFFICULTY LEVEL: ★

YIELD: Serves 32; Makes 2 cups

COST PER SERVING: $

CALORIES: 6

FAT: 0 g

PROTEIN: 0 g

SODIUM: 1 mg

FIBER: 1 g

CARBOHYDRATES: 1 g

SUGAR: 0 g

The homey, comforting scent of savory herbs is welcome anytime of year, but especially during festive holiday times when they accompany roasted meats and various comfort foods. Having this blend on hand will simplify your holiday cooking and provide a blend you'll reach for all year-round.

½ **cup sage**

½ **cup thyme**

¼ **cup rosemary**

2 tablespoons dried onion flakes

2 tablespoons parsley

2 tablespoons marjoram

2 tablespoons dehydrated bell peppers

1 tablespoon Greek oregano

1 tablespoon savory

Whisk everything together in a small bowl and store in an airtight container for up to 6 months.

Greek Herb Blend

HANDS-ON: 5 minutes

INACTIVE: none

READY IN: 5 minutes

DIFFICULTY LEVEL: ★

YIELD: Serves 8; Makes ½ cup

COST PER SERVING: $

CALORIES: 10

FAT: 0 g

PROTEIN: 0.5 g

SODIUM: 590 mg

FIBER: 1 g

CARBOHYDRATES: 2 g

SUGAR: 0 g

This easy-to-make Greek herb blend uses a mix of traditional dried herbs and spices that capture the flavors and aromas of the Greek isles. Try it over grilled meats, in rice pilaf, or stirred into yogurt to create a delicious vegetable dip.

3 tablespoons Greek oregano

2 tablespoons thyme

1 tablespoon onion flakes

1 teaspoon garlic powder

1 teaspoon black pepper

1 tablespoon basil

1 teaspoon cinnamon

1 teaspoon grated nutmeg

2 teaspoons salt

Whisk everything together in a small bowl and store in an airtight container for up to 6 months.

Tandoori Blend

HANDS-ON: 5 minutes

INACTIVE: none

READY IN: 5 minutes

DIFFICULTY LEVEL: ★

YIELD: Serves 8; Makes ½ cup

COST PER SERVING: $

CALORIES: 19

FAT: 0.5 g

PROTEIN: 0.5 g

SODIUM: 3 mg

FIBER: 1.5 g

CARBOHYDRATES: 4 g

SUGAR: 0 g

Tandoori is a traditional cooking method from India and Central Asia that first marinates meat or vegetables in spices and yogurt, then cooks them at very high temperatures in a clay oven. The resulting dishes are mouth-watering and tender. Rub this spice blend on meat or vegetables for a taste of the Silk Road and you won't be disappointed.

1 tablespoon garlic powder

1 tablespoon ground ginger

1 tablespoon ground coriander

1 tablespoon turmeric

1 tablespoon ground cumin

1 tablespoon freshly ground black pepper

½ tablespoon cayenne pepper

½ tablespoon nutmeg

½ tablespoon cinnamon

Whisk everything in a small bowl and store in an airtight container for up to 6 months.

Seafood Blend

HANDS-ON: 10 minutes

INACTIVE: none

READY IN: 10 minutes

DIFFICULTY LEVEL: ★

YIELD: Serves 8; Makes ½ cup

COST PER SERVING: $

CALORIES: 14

FAT: 0.5 g

PROTEIN: 0.5 g

SODIUM: 1,103 mg

FIBER: 1 g

CARBOHYDRATES: 2.5 g

SUGAR: 0 g

This popular blend accompanies crab and shrimp especially well, but can be used to flavor pretty much anything from popcorn to French fries. If you remove or reduce the celery salt, it can be used as a healthy salt substitute, as well.

6 bay leaves

4 teaspoons celery salt

1 tablespoon dry mustard

1 tablespoon black pepper

2 teaspoons sweet or smoked paprika

2 teaspoons celery seeds

1 teaspoon nutmeg

1 teaspoon ginger

¼ teaspoon ground cloves

¼ teaspoon ground mace

¼ teaspoon ground cardamom

¼ teaspoon ground allspice

Dash of crushed red pepper flakes

1. Place all ingredients in a spice grinder or old coffee grinder and pulse until ground into a coarse powder.

2. Store in an airtight container for up to 6 months.

Pumpkin Pie Spice

HANDS-ON: 5 minutes

INACTIVE: none

READY IN: 5 minutes

DIFFICULTY LEVEL: ★

YIELD: Serves 8; Makes ½ cup

COST PER SERVING: $

CALORIES: 14

FAT: 0.5 g

PROTEIN: 0 g

SODIUM: 1 mg

FIBER: 2 g

CARBOHYDRATES: 4 g

SUGAR: 0 g

When you're whipping up a pumpkin pie for a holiday gathering or just like to have a blend of warm, autumnal spices on hand, this pumpkin pie spice is your answer. It's great not only on winter squash (like pumpkin), but on top of coffee, apple slices, or on ice cream. It can even stand in as a healthy sugar substitute in some instances.

¼ cup cinnamon
1 teaspoon ground ginger
2 teaspoons nutmeg
2 teaspoons allspice powder
½ teaspoon ground cloves

Whisk everything together in a small bowl. Store in an airtight container for up to 6 months.

Lemon-Pepper Seasoning

HANDS-ON: 10 minutes

INACTIVE: 2 hours

READY IN: 2 hours

DIFFICULTY LEVEL: ★

YIELD: Serves 16; Makes 1 cup

COST PER SERVING: $

CALORIES: 12

FAT: 0 g

PROTEIN: 0.5 g

SODIUM: 1,668 mg

FIBER: 1 g

CARBOHYDRATES: 3.5 g

SUGAR: 0.5 g

Lemon-pepper seasoning is a great all-purpose seasoning and can be used anywhere you use salt. Try it on everything: grilled meats, roasted fish, salad dressings—you name it!

6 lemons, zested
6 tablespoons black peppercorns
4 tablespoons salt

1. Place the lemon zest on a baking sheet. Set in the oven on the lowest setting and leave until completely dried, about 1 hour. Cool completely. Grind with the peppercorns and salt in a food processor or spice mill until well mixed.

2. Store in an airtight container for up to 3 months.

CHAPTER 9

Beverages

There's nothing like sipping your own homemade ginger ale or lemonade on a hot summer day, and it's delightfully satisfying to serve up old-fashioned, homemade eggnog or old-world mulled wine at a winter holiday party. The recipes in this chapter will provide you with the most common drinks you'll find at the grocery store. Instead of processed sodas and drink mixes laden with high fructose corn syrup and chemical additives, you'll find all-natural beverages that can be made in a pinch with readily available ingredients. You'll never again have to worry about what exactly you're sipping on when you pour yourself a cup of homemade tea, hot chocolate, and even almond milk!

Ginger Ale

True, old-fashioned ginger ale is made using yeast like a lot of other ales. But yeast ales takes time to brew. This soda syrup substitute is quick and easy and can be made at home without very many ingredients. You don't have to wait for two days for the fermentation to finish, so you can enjoy it whenever you'd like. It's very refreshing on a hot summer day.

HANDS-ON: 10 minutes

INACTIVE: 1 hour

READY IN: 1 hour

DIFFICULTY LEVEL: ★

YIELD: Serves 6; Makes 3 cups syrup

COST PER SERVING: $

CALORIES: 135

FAT: 0 g

PROTEIN: 0 g

SODIUM: 16 mg

FIBER: 0 g

CARBOHYDRATES: 34 g

SUGAR: 33 g

2 cups water

1 cup unrefined cane sugar

¼ cup freshly shredded ginger

Juice of ½ a lemon or lime

9 cups sparkling water

1. Place the water and the sugar in a saucepan and bring to a boil, stirring to dissolve the sugar. As soon as the sugar is dissolved, remove from the heat and add in the shredded ginger. Cover and let sit until completely cool.

2. When cool, strain out the ginger, stir in the lemon or lime juice, and then transfer syrup to an airtight container and keep refrigerated until ready to use, up to 2 weeks.

3. Serve 1 part syrup to 3 parts sparkling water.

Cola Syrup

This recipe has all the flavor of cola, but is far lighter and much more refreshing than the store-bought original. It is thought that Coca-Cola's original recipe was far lighter than the dark, syrupy version we have today, so perhaps this homemade version gives us a glimpse into what the inventor of cola had in mind. There are two difficult-to-find ingredients in this recipe, but you can definitely make the recipe without them. The bitter orange gives a hint of the flavor present in Coca-Cola, and kola nut provides caffeine. Earl Grey tea gives a hint of color to the soda and the bergamot mimics one of cola's distinct flavors, neroli, but definitely stick to the amount recommended here, as the Earl Grey will easily take over the other flavors.

HANDS-ON: 30 minutes

INACTIVE: 1½ hours

READY IN: 2 hours

DIFFICULTY LEVEL: ★ ★ ★

YIELD: Serves 6; Makes 5 cups syrup

COST PER SERVING: $ $ $ $

CALORIES: 274

FAT: 0.5 g

PROTEIN: 0.3 g

SODIUM: 28 mg

FIBER: 1 g

CARBOHYDRATES: 69 g

SUGAR: 67 g

3 cups water

Orange zest from 4 large oranges

Lime zest from 4 limes

Lemon zest from 2 lemons

2 tablespoons dried bitter orange peel (optional)

1 tablespoon freshly grated gingerroot

½ teaspoon freshly grated nutmeg

3 tablespoons dried lavender flowers

2 tablespoons kola nut (optional)

2 tablespoons coriander seed

1 cinnamon stick

1 star anise

2 cups unrefined cane sugar

2 teaspoons vanilla extract

Lime juice from 2 limes

¼ cup very strongly brewed Earl Grey tea, preferably double bergamot (optional)

½ teaspoon citric acid

20 cups sparkling water

1. In a small saucepan, combine the water, zests, bitter orange, ginger, nutmeg, lavender, kola nut, coriander, cinnamon, and star anise. Bring to a boil over medium-high heat; then remove from heat and let steep for 1 hour, covered.

2. Strain through a cheesecloth; then return flavored water to a large saucepan and add sugar, making sure that there are at least 3 cups of flavored water (add plain water to make up the difference, if needed).

3. Bring to a steady simmer and stir to dissolve sugar. Remove from heat as soon as the sugar is dissolved; then stir in the vanilla extract, lime juice, brewed tea, and citric acid. Let cool; then transfer syrup to an airtight container and keep refrigerated until ready to use, up to 2 weeks.

4. Serve 1 part syrup to 4 parts sparkling water.

Root Beer Syrup

The original root beer was exactly that—a brew made from the dried roots of a number of plants, shrubs, and trees. The flavors we recognize today as the hallmarks of root beer are sarsaparilla and sassafrass, so they play center stage in this soda syrup recipe. And by making this as an easy soda syrup rather than a traditionally fermented root beer, you can enjoy your bubbly drink within a few hours rather than waiting for several days for it to brew.

HANDS-ON: 20 minutes

INACTIVE: 2½ hours

READY IN: 3 hours

DIFFICULTY LEVEL: ★ ★ ★

YIELD: Serves 6; Makes 5 cups syrup

COST PER SERVING: $ $ $ $

CALORIES: 334

FAT: 1 g

PROTEIN: 1.5 g

SODIUM: 41 mg

FIBER: 2 g

CARBOHYDRATES: 83 g

SUGAR: 74 g

3 cups water

½ cup dried sassafras root bark

¼ cup sarsaparilla root

½ cup dried mint

6 star anise pods

1 (1") piece ginger, grated

1 cinnamon stick

1½ tablespoons licorice root powder, or 2 long licorice root sticks (optional)

2 cups unrefined cane sugar

¼ cup molasses

1 teaspoon vanilla extract

20 cups sparkling water

1.   Place the water along with the sassafras, sarsaparilla, mint, star anise, ginger, cinnamon, and licorice root in a large saucepan and bring to a boil over medium-high heat. Remove pot from heat, cover, and let steep for 2 hours.

2.   Strain through a cheesecloth; then return flavored water to a large saucepan and add sugar and molasses. Make sure there are at least 3 cups of liquid (add plain water to make up the difference, if needed).

3.   Bring to a steady simmer and stir to dissolve sugar and molasses. Remove from heat as soon as the sugar is dissolved; then stir in the vanilla extract. Let cool; then transfer syrup to an airtight container and keep refrigerated until ready to use, up to 2 weeks.

4.   Serve 1 part syrup to 4 parts sparkling water.

Almond Milk

Almond milk in the store has a number of stabilizers added to make it shelf stable; fresh almond milk is rich in comparison. Even if you aren't in need of a dairy-free milk alternative, almond milk is so creamy and luscious that it's worth a try. Try it slightly warmed with maple syrup, vanilla extract, cinnamon, and nutmeg.

HANDS-ON: 5 minutes

INACTIVE: 4–6 hours

READY IN: 6 hours

DIFFICULTY LEVEL: ★

YIELD: Serves 8; Makes 4 cups

COST PER SERVING: $ $

CALORIES: 68

FAT: 6 g

PROTEIN: 3 g

SODIUM: 22 mg

FIBER: 1.5 g

CARBOHYDRATES: 2.5 g

SUGAR: 0.5 g

1 cup raw almonds

4 cups fresh water

¹⁄₁₆ teaspoon salt

1. Place the raw almonds in a large bowl and cover with warm water. Let sit for 4–6 hours.

2. Drain off the soaking water and place the almonds in a blender. Add 1 cup of the fresh water; then blend until very smooth, about 1 minute. Slowly add the remaining 3 cups of fresh water (or reduce the amount for a richer milk).

3. Sprinkle in the salt; then strain the milk into a large bowl through a fine-mesh sieve or a nut milk bag. Reserve the nut pulp, either to blend with fresh water for a second batch of weaker milk, or for other recipes. Store in an airtight container for up to 3 days.

Hot Chocolate Mix

Nothing makes a cold, dreary day better more than a cup of steaming hot chocolate. Store-brand versions often contain unidentifiable ingredients, so you never know what's in your cup, but now, with this recipe, you don't have to worry. Filled with only wholesome ingredients and the flavor you've always loved, this recipe is perfect for rainy days or right after a snowstorm.

HANDS-ON: 10 minutes

INACTIVE: none

READY IN: 10 minutes

DIFFICULTY LEVEL: ★

YIELD: Serves 24; Makes 1 quart dry mix

COST PER SERVING: $

GF V DF EF

CALORIES: 69

FAT: 2.5 g

PROTEIN: 1.5 g

SODIUM: 198 mg

FIBER: 2 g

CARBOHYDRATES: 14 g

SUGAR: 10 g

2 cups powdered sugar

2 cups cocoa powder

40 grams (¼ cup) cocoa butter, cut into small pieces, or white chocolate chips

2 teaspoons salt

1 vanilla bean (optional)

1. Place powdered sugar, cocoa powder, cocoa butter, and salt in a food processor and pulse until everything is finely powdered. Scrape in the seeds from a vanilla bean and set aside. If you'd like extra "vanilla-y" flavor, place the split bean in the storage container along with the hot cocoa mix.

2. To serve, place 2 heaping tablespoons in a large mug and pour boiling water or hot milk over. Stir until dissolved. Sip and enjoy.

3. Store mix in an airtight container for up to 6 months.

Classic Eggnog

Eggnog is one of winter's delights and since the Middle Ages has served as a toast to prosperity and good health. The saccarine supermarket varieties today don't hold a candle to the "real thing" in either flavor or nutrition and are often stuffed full of chemical additives, so this winter, whip up a batch of this classic drink and raise a toast to a healthy, blessed new year.

Oh, and an important note about raw eggs: raw egg yolks are packed full of fantastic nutrition, including caretenoids, essential fatty acids, a host of vitamins, minerals, and folic acid, just to name a few. However, conventional store-bought eggs also tend to sit around for a few weeks before they're sold, so they can be a breeding ground for bacteria and should NOT be consumed raw, especially if you're pregnant or dealing with illness. Thus, if you're going to use raw egg yolks, this is one time when it's important to source out fresh eggs from chickens raised on pasture (or even in a backyard!). If you don't know where to look, see the Appendix at the back of this book for a few ideas.

HANDS-ON: 5 minutes

INACTIVE: 1–12 hours

READY IN: 1 hour

DIFFICULTY LEVEL: ★

YIELD: Serves 5; Makes 5 cups

COST PER SERVING: $ $ $

GF V

CALORIES: 470

FAT: 40 g

PROTEIN: 9 g

SODIUM: 80 mg

FIBER: 1 g

CARBOHYDRATES: 19 g

SUGAR: 13 g

1½ cups milk

2 cups cream

9 egg yolks, as fresh as possible

¼ cup maple syrup (or more, to taste)

1 teaspoon real vanilla extract

1 tablespoon ground cinnamon

¼–½ teaspoon freshly ground nutmeg

1. Place all ingredients in a blender or a large bowl. Blend or whisk until very smooth and a bit frothy.

2. Set in the refrigerator for at least 1 hour and preferably overnight to chill thoroughly and allow flavors to blend.

3. Serve chilled. Store in the refrigerator for up to 2 days.

Honey-Sweetened Lemonade

HANDS-ON: 15 minutes

INACTIVE: 2 hours

READY IN: 2 hours

DIFFICULTY LEVEL: ★

YIELD: Serves 8; Makes 2½ quarts

COST PER SERVING: $

GF V DF EF

CALORIES: 145

FAT: 0 g

PROTEIN: 1 g

SODIUM: 9 mg

FIBER: 1.5 g

CARBOHYDRATES: 40 g

SUGAR: 36 g

There is nothing more refreshing on a hot summer day than lemonade, but most mixes are chock-full of processed sugars. This homemade version of the classic drink uses honey as the sweetener to cut out a lot of the unnecessary sweetness, but retains the bright flavor you crave.

8 cups water
1 cup honey
8 lemons, juiced

1. Place half the water in a large saucepan and heat over medium heat. Add the honey and continue to heat until honey is completely dissolved.

2. Pour the honey water and remaining water into a large jar and add the juice from the lemons. Stir well and chill. Store in an airtight container in the refrigerator for up to 5 days.

Sleepytime Tea

HANDS-ON: 5 minutes

INACTIVE: none

READY IN: 5 minutes

DIFFICULTY LEVEL: ★

YIELD: Serves 20; Makes 1¼ cups

COST PER SERVING: $

GF V DF EF

CALORIES: 4

FAT: 0 g

PROTEIN: 0 g

SODIUM: 2 mg

FIBER: 0 g

CARBOHYDRATES: 1 g

SUGAR: 0 g

When you or your child need help settling at the end of the day, this is a wonderful, calming blend to help you relax and let the day slowly melt away.

½ cup chamomile blossoms
½ cup valerian root
¼ cup mint

1. Combine chamomile, valerian, and mint in a bowl and stir to mix well.

2. Store in an airtight container for up to one year.

3. Brew by placing 1 tablespoon of tea in a reusable tea bag and placing the tea bag in a cup. Fill the cup with freshly boiled water. Steep for 4–6 minutes; then remove tea.

North African Mint Tea

HANDS-ON: 5 minutes

INACTIVE: none

READY IN: 5 minutes

DIFFICULTY LEVEL: ★

YIELD: Serves 16; Makes 1 cup

COST PER SERVING: $ $

CALORIES: 25

FAT: 0 g

PROTEIN: 1 g

SODIUM: 2 mg

FIBER: 0 g

CARBOHYDRATES: 5 g

SUGAR: 0 g

Typically, Moroccan mint tea has just mint and green tea, but this is a jazzed-up version that—ironically—can be more calming. If you want a simpler version, just mix the peppermint and green tea.

40 dry cardamom pods
½ cup dried peppermint
⅛ cup any Japanese-style green tea (Hojicha and sencha being favorites)
1 teaspoon fennel seed (optional)
10 whole cloves
20 black peppercorns

1. Combine all ingredients in a bowl and stir to mix well.

2. Store in an airtight container for up to one year.

3. Brew by placing 1 tablespoon of tea in a reusable tea bag and placing the tea bag in a cup. Fill the cup with freshly boiled water. Steep for 3–5 minutes; then remove tea.

Sniffles 9-1-1

HANDS-ON: 5 minutes

INACTIVE: none

READY IN: 5 minutes

DIFFICULTY LEVEL: ★

YIELD: Serves 28; Makes 1¾ cups

COST PER SERVING: $

CALORIES: 16

FAT: 0 g

PROTEIN: 1 g

SODIUM: 6 mg

FIBER: 1.5 g

CARBOHYDRATES: 3.5 g

SUGAR: 0 g

During rainy seasons and the winter, it can be difficult to rid yourself of nasty colds, or at the very least, the sniffles. This tea will not only help you feel better; it will actively promote healing due to the elder flowers and echinacea. Elderberry has been clinically proven to ward off multiple strains of influenza, and echinacea provides a healthy boost to the immune system.

½ cup dried peppermint
½ cup elderberry flowers
2 tablespoons juniper berries
1 tablespoon fresh or dried orange peel
½ cup coarsely chopped echinacea root

1. Combine all ingredients in a bowl and stir to mix well.

2. Store in an airtight container for up to one year.

3. Brew by placing 1 tablespoon of herbs in a reusable tea bag and placing the tea bag in a cup. Fill the cup with freshly boiled water. Steep for 4–7 minutes; then remove tea.

Swedish Mulled Wine

The Swedes—those northern clime–loving folk—came up with one of the best recipes for mulled wine. Sipping this syrupy, aromatic wine is like coming home to a crackling fire—it will warm you from your head to your toes; it will make you glad for the moment; and it will fill your heart with longing for the people and places you've loved.

HANDS-ON: 10 minutes

INACTIVE: 1–2 hours

READY IN: 1 hour

DIFFICULTY LEVEL: ★

YIELD: Serves 8; Makes 1 quart

COST PER SERVING: $ $ $ $

CALORIES: 385

FAT: 7 g

PROTEIN: 4 g

SODIUM: 12 mg

FIBER: 4.5 g

CARBOHYDRATES: 44 g

SUGAR: 33 g

3 cups full-bodied red wine

1 cup vodka

1 cup unrefined cane sugar or other granulated sugar

20 cardamom pods, crushed

10 cloves

1 orange peel

1 cinnamon stick

1 (2") piece fresh gingerroot, cut into 5–6 coins

½ cup raisins

1 star anise (optional)

1 cup blanched almonds

1. Stir together all ingredients, except for the almonds, in a large, heavy-bottomed pot. Heat gently over medium-low heat and let it mull, covered, for at least 1–2 hours before serving.

2. To serve, strain well and ladle into serving cups or mugs, adding 1–2 almonds to each one. Store any leftover wine in the refrigerator in an airtight container for up to 5 days.

CHAPTER 10

Desserts and Sweets

No pantry would be complete without a few desserts hiding away in it. Whether you need to mix up a quick batch of cookies for a bake sale, are craving an ice cream sundae, or have midnight cravings for a chocolate cake smothered in decadent chocolate frosting, this chapter has just what you need to fulfill that sweet tooth. Best of all, these guilty pleasures aren't as bad for you as their store-bought counterparts, so even if you get an insatiable urge to munch on something sweet, you're better off taking a bite out of these all-natural treats.

Yellow Cake Mix

Cake mixes from the store have a host of additives and preservatives, but thankfully, it's easy to whip up a dry mix at home that you can have on hand for whenever you need to make a cake or cupcakes on short notice. This yellow cake is a favorite for birthday parties, lazy Sunday afternoons, or whenever you feel the need for cake.

HANDS-ON: 15 minutes

INACTIVE: 30 minutes

READY IN: 45 minutes

DIFFICULTY LEVEL: ★ ★

YIELD: Serves 24; Makes one 9" × 13" cake, two 9" round cakes, 24 cupcakes, or 36 mini-cupcakes

COST PER SERVING: $ $

CALORIES: 155

FAT: 7 g

PROTEIN: 2.5 g

SODIUM: 184 mg

FIBER: 0.5 g

CARBOHYDRATES: 20 g

SUGAR: 11 g

2¼ cups all-purpose flour

1¼ cups unrefined cane sugar

3½ teaspoons baking powder

1 teaspoon sea salt

½ cup palm shortening or cold butter, cubed

1¼ cups milk

¼ cup coconut oil, melted

1 tablespoon vanilla extract

3 large eggs

1. Sift together the flour, sugar, baking powder, and salt.

2. Add the palm shortening or cold butter cubes and rub them into the flour mixture until the entire mixture looks like fine crumbs.

3. Store the dry cake mixture in an airtight container for up to 6 months if you used palm shortening, or for up to 2 weeks if you used butter.

4. To make the cake, mix the milk, coconut oil, vanilla, and eggs into the dry cake mix. Mix well and beat for 2 minutes.

5. Scrape the batter into greased pans and bake at 350°F for the estimated time listed below until a toothpick comes out clean or until the cake springs back when touched lightly near the center. Estimated bake times:

- 9" × 13" pan: 32–36 minutes
- 9" cake pans: 27–31 minutes
- Cupcakes: 17–20 minutes
- Mini-cupcakes: 11–14 minutes

6. Let cool in the pan for about 15 minutes; then invert onto a rack to cool completely. Store cake or cupcakes in an airtight resealable plastic bag or other airtight container for up for 5 days.

Chocolate Cake Mix

Chocolate covers a multitude of sins, and it's the perfect foil for hiding healthy ingredients as well! Using whole-wheat flour instead of all-purpose actually enhances the chocolate flavor by adding a nutty undertone. The same logic works for the coffee grounds—you won't notice their texture and using coffee is an old trick for making chocolate even "chocolate-ier."

HANDS-ON: 15 minutes

INACTIVE: 30 minutes

READY IN: 45 minutes

DIFFICULTY LEVEL: ★ ★

YIELD: Serves 24; Makes one 9" ×13" cake, two 9" round cakes, 24 cupcakes, or 36 mini-cupcakes

COST PER SERVING: $ $

CALORIES: 164

FAT: 10 g

PROTEIN: 3 g

SODIUM: 158 mg

FIBER: 2.5 g

CARBOHYDRATES: 18 g

SUGAR: 9 g

2 cups whole-wheat or spelt flour

1 cup unrefined cane sugar or coconut sugar

1 cup cocoa

2 teaspoons baking powder

1 teaspoon baking soda

½ teaspoon salt

1 tablespoon finely ground coffee

¼ cup palm shortening

1⅓ cups milk

⅔ cup coconut oil, melted

3 eggs

1. Sift the flour, sugar, cocoa, baking powder, baking soda, salt, and coffee into a large bowl.

2. Blend in the shortening with a pastry blender or your fingertips, as if you were making biscuits. Blend until no lumps remain and the entire mixture looks like fine crumbs. Store the dry cake mix in an airtight container for up to 6 months.

3. To make the cake, add the milk, oil, and eggs to the cake mix in a large bowl and beat well.

4. Scrape the batter into greased pans and bake at 350°F for the allotted time (estimated bake times follow). The mix makes one 9" × 13" cake, two 9" round cakes, 24 cupcakes, or 3 dozen mini-cupcakes. Estimated bake times:

- 9" × 13" pan: 35–38 minutes
- 9" cake pans: 30–33 minutes
- Cupcakes: 19–22 minutes
- Mini-cupcakes: 12–15 minutes

5. Let cool in the pan for about 15 minutes; then invert onto a rack to cool completely. Store cake or cupcakes in an airtight resealable plastic bag or other airtight container for up for 5 days.

Chocolate Pudding

This chocolate pudding recipe is just as easy as mixing up the boxed version! Be sure to whisk well if lumps form, or strain it through a strainer once you're done. For a dairy-free version, feel free to use milk substitutes, such as almond milk or coconut milk. However, try to avoid rice milk and skim milk, merely because such extremely low-fat liquids will not thicken well.

HANDS-ON: 30 minutes

INACTIVE: 1 hour

READY IN: 1½ hours

DIFFICULTY LEVEL: ★ ★ ★

YIELD: Serves 6; Makes 6 cups

COST PER SERVING: $ $ $

CALORIES: 420

FAT: 16 g

PROTEIN: 7 g

SODIUM: 173 mg

FIBER: 2 g

CARBOHYDRATES: 66 g

SUGAR: 54 g

4 cups cold whole milk, almond milk, or coconut milk, divided

¾ cup sugar

¼ teaspoon salt

½ cup cornstarch or tapioca starch

8 ounces dark chocolate, coarsely chopped

2 teaspoons vanilla extract

Flavoring of choice: ¼ teaspoon cinnamon, 1 dash of hot sauce, ½ teaspoon mint extract, or 1 tablespoon orange liqueur (optional)

1. Place 3 cups of the milk, along with the sugar and salt, in a large, heavy-bottomed saucepan. Heat slowly over medium-low heat, stirring occasionally, until the milk is steaming and the sugar is dissolved, about 10 minutes.

2. Meanwhile, place the starch in a bowl and drizzle in the remaining cup of milk while whisking to create first a slurry and then a fully dissolved milk/starch mixture.

3. Pour the milk/starch mixture into the hot milk and whisk to mix well. Let it cook, stirring occasionally, until it is once again hot and the mixture has thickened noticeably, 7–9 minutes. Remember that the mixture will continue to thicken as it cools.

4. Add in the chocolate, stirring often, until the chocolate is melted and the pudding is smooth. Stir in the vanilla and your flavoring of choice and spoon into serving dishes. Place plastic wrap directly on the pudding to prevent a skin from forming (if one does, you can just pull it off) and place in the refrigerator for at least 1 hour before serving.

5. Store in an airtight container in the refrigerator for up to 3 days.

Almond Paste

This method of making almond paste is simple and stunning. The recipe tastes like it came straight off the confectioner's worktable in the Old World, and it's just the right texture to knead and shape as desired. The ratio of sugar and honey here provides the best texture and best moisture for the paste.

HANDS-ON: 20 minutes

INACTIVE: 1 hour

READY IN: 1 hour 20 minutes

DIFFICULTY LEVEL: ★ ★

YIELD: Serves 16; Makes 4 cups

COST PER SERVING: $ $

GF   DF EF

CALORIES: 181

FAT: 9 g

PROTEIN: 4 g

SODIUM: 1 mg

FIBER: 2 g

CARBOHYDRATES: 22 g

SUGAR: 19 g

3¼ cups whole, blanched almonds

1⅛ cups unrefined cane sugar

¼ cup honey

7 tablespoons water

1 tablespoon almond extract

1. If your almonds aren't preblanched, blanch them.

2. Place the almonds in a food processor and grind until they are the size of very coarsely ground coffee. Let sit until the sugar mixture is ready.

3. Place the sugar, honey, and water in a medium saucepan and bring to a full, rolling boil over medium-high heat. While it's still boiling, pour the syrup over the almonds; then process until smooth, which usually takes 5–10 minutes. At some point in the first few minutes of grinding, add the almond extract through the feed tube so that it gets thoroughly worked into the dough.

4. Remove the almond paste from the processor and wrap it tightly in plastic wrap. Place in the refrigerator until fully chilled; then use as desired. Store in the refrigerator in an airtight container for 2 weeks.

HOW TO BLANCH ALMONDS

Bring a large saucepan of water to a boil; then add any amount of raw almonds. Let the almonds simmer for about 60 seconds; then drain them, run them under cold tap water to stop the cooking process, and completely cool them. Pour them out onto towels and pat them dry. At this point, you should notice the skins beginning to shrivel, so squeeze and rub each almond gently until the skins begin to peel off. Use the blanched almonds immediately, or store them in an airtight container in the freezer for up to 6 months.

Honey Caramel Sauce

This Honey Caramel Sauce is a sweet addition to any pantry! It's exquisite drizzled into apple cider in the fall, poured over a fruit crumble in the late summer, or just eaten straight off the spoon. Caramel is typically made with sugar, but can be a bit tricky due to the fickle nature of sugar, so this recipe prepares it with honey instead for a slightly more reliable version for first-time caramel makers. If for some reason it seizes and turns into a grainy mass rather than the silky smooth sauce you're envisioning, just schedule a movie night with good friends, serve your crumbled caramel creation tossed with almonds and popcorn, and none of your efforts will have gone to waste.

HANDS-ON: 20 minutes

INACTIVE: 1 hour

READY IN: 20 minutes

DIFFICULTY LEVEL: ★

YIELD: Serves 8; Makes 1 cup

COST PER SERVING: $ $

CALORIES: 173

FAT: 8 g

PROTEIN: 0.5 g

SODIUM: 154 mg

FIBER: 0 g

CARBOHYDRATES: 26 g

SUGAR: 26 g

¾ **cup honey**

½ **cup heavy cream**

2 **tablespoons butter**

½ **teaspoon coarse unrefined sea salt**

1.   For the sauce, place all ingredients in a heavy-bottomed saucepan and bring to a boil over medium-high heat. Keep at a steady boil for 8–10 minutes, whisking regularly.

2.   Reduce heat to medium and continue to simmer until the mixture just begins to coat the back of a spoon and begins to deepen in color to a dark golden brown, about 5 minutes. (If you want to get technical, pull it off the heat at 230°F, just before it reaches the softball candy stage.)

3.   Drizzle immediately into hot cider, or pour into a jar and let cool, about 1 hour. Store in the refrigerator for up to 2 weeks.

Chocolate Chips

Chocolate Chips are actually super easy to make, but make sure to keep your tools completely dry, as even a small amount of water can make them turn from smooth to grainy. Although once they're gooey and delicious in a cookie, who can tell the difference?

HANDS-ON: 20 minutes

INACTIVE: 1 hour

READY IN: 1½ hours

DIFFICULTY LEVEL: ★ ★ ★

YIELD: Serves 16; Makes 4 cups

COST PER SERVING: $ $

CALORIES: 162

FAT: 14 g

PROTEIN: 1 g

SODIUM: 1 mg

FIBER: 2 g

CARBOHYDRATES: 9.5 g

SUGAR: 6 g

1 cup (8 ounces) cocoa butter

½ cup cane sugar or honey

1 cup cocoa powder

1 tablespoon vanilla extract

1 tablespoon brewed espresso (optional)

1. Prepare a double boiler or place a large nonreactive bowl over a pot of simmering water, preferably covering the rim of the pot completely so that no water can splash into the bowl. Add the cocoa butter and the sugar. (If you are using honey, be sure not to add cold honey to cocoa butter that is already warm—either add hot honey or melt them together.)

2. Once the cocoa butter has melted completely and the sugar is dissolved, whisk in the cocoa powder a small amount at a time and stir until there are no lumps. Add the vanilla extract and the coffee and whisk until smooth.

3. Pour onto a parchment paper–lined baking pan and let harden at room temperature, about 1 hour.

4. Chop into small pieces and store in a cool, dark place in an airtight container for up to 6 months.

Chocolate Syrup

Whether it's for pouring over ice cream or for stirring into chocolate milk, this chocolate syrup hits the spot every time.

HANDS-ON: 10 minutes

INACTIVE: none

READY IN: 10 minutes

DIFFICULTY LEVEL: ★

YIELD: Serves 8; Makes 2 cups

COST PER SERVING: $

GF V V DF EF

CALORIES: 55

FAT: 0.5 g

PROTEIN: 0.5 g

SODIUM: 19 mg

FIBER: 1 g

CARBOHYDRATES: 14 g

SUGAR: 12 g

½ cup cocoa powder

¾ cup water

1 cup sugar or honey

⅛ teaspoon salt

1 teaspoon vanilla extract

1. Place the cocoa powder, water, sugar, and salt in a large, heavy-bottomed saucepan and whisk to combine well.

2. Turn on the heat to medium and whisk until smooth. Bring to a gentle boil over medium heat and let it simmer uncovered steadily for 6–7 minutes, stirring often. Once the mixture thickens a bit, remove from the heat and then add the vanilla extract.

3. Pour into an airtight storage container, such as a Mason jar or a leftover chocolate syrup bottle. Note that the syrup will still be quite thin, but it will thicken as it cools.

4. Store in the refrigerator for 3–4 weeks.

Chocolate Ice Cream Shell

Melted chocolate in any form will harden when it hits cold ice cream, but the "magic" in this shell is that the chocolate hardens in a thin, smooth shell rather than glopping up in a ball. Children of all ages have been delighted by this simple pleasure since it appeared on the market several decades ago. It turns out making it at home is incredibly easy, but you can still keep this recipe as your magician's secret, if you'd like. The only difficulty is choosing which chocolate to melt down. Choose a high-quality brand you already enjoy eating and this recipe will be sure to please.

HANDS-ON: 10 minutes

INACTIVE: none

READY IN: 10 minutes

DIFFICULTY LEVEL: ★

YIELD: Serves 10; Makes 1¼ cups

COST PER SERVING: $

CALORIES: 190

FAT: 17 g

PROTEIN: 1 g

SODIUM: 31 mg

FIBER: 1 g

CARBOHYDRATES: 10 g

SUGAR: 9 g

½ cup coconut oil

6 ounces dark chocolate

1 tablespoon sunflower oil

⅛ teaspoon salt

1 teaspoon vanilla extract

1.   Melt the coconut oil in a large saucepan; then add the dark chocolate, sunflower oil, and salt.

2.   When the chocolate is melted, remove from the heat and whisk until the mixture is completely smooth. Stir in the vanilla extract and whisk again.

3.   Pour into an old squeeze bottle or small glass jars and store at room temperature for up to 3 months.

Fruit Curd

Fruit curd adds a touch of class to anything: custards, cakes, or even just spooned over yogurt on a lazy weekend morning. Traditional curd is made of citrus juice, so be sure to strain it well to make it completely pulp-free. If you wish to explore a less juicy fruit option, such as mango or kiwi, be sure to purée the fruit extremely well and pass it through a sieve to remove any solids.

HANDS-ON: 25 minutes

INACTIVE: 1 hour

READY IN: 1½ hours

DIFFICULTY LEVEL: ★ ★ ★

YIELD: Serves 8; Makes 2 cups

COST PER SERVING: $ $

GF

CALORIES: 130

FAT: 9 g

PROTEIN: 1.5 g

SODIUM: 42 mg

FIBER: 0 g

CARBOHYDRATES: 10 g

SUGAR: 10 g

5 tablespoons butter, soft

¼ cup honey

4 large egg yolks, at room temperature

⅛ teaspoon salt

½ cup freshly squeezed fruit juice or fruit pulp, strained

1. Cream the butter in the bowl of an electric mixer. Add the honey and beat until fluffy and light. Add the yolks one at a time, beating well to incorporate after each addition. Sprinkle in the salt; then reduce the speed to low and gradually add the fruit juice.

2. Place the bowl on top of a simmering pan of water. Heat slowly, whisking constantly, until the butter melts and the mixture is thick enough to coat the back of a spoon, about 10 minutes. Cover and chill in the refrigerator until firm, at least 1 hour. Keep in mind that your curd will thicken substantially as it cools.

3. Store in an airtight container in the refrigerator for up to 2 weeks, or in the freezer for up to 2 months.

Ice Cream

On a hot day when the mercury is rising, there is nothing better than a creamy, frozen treat. Considering the store-bought versions include hydrogenated oils and artificial flavorings, making ice cream at home is a sure-fire hit. Not only does it taste worlds better than store-bought varieties, but with its nourishing cream and eggs, it's actually a healthy treat—in moderation of course! If you choose to use the raw egg yolks in this recipe, use only very fresh eggs that were raised on pasture, since this makes a vast difference both in nutrition and in safety. Of course, you can always go without them, as the recipe comes out just as delicious!

HANDS-ON: 5 minutes

INACTIVE: 2½ hours

READY IN: 2½ hours

DIFFICULTY LEVEL: ★

YIELD: Serves 6; Makes 1½ quarts

COST PER SERVING: $ $

GF **V**

CALORIES: 370

FAT: 30 g

PROTEIN: 3 g

SODIUM: 74 mg

FIBER: 0 g

CARBOHYDRATES: 22 g

SUGAR: 18 g

2 cups heavy cream

1 cup whole milk

½ cup maple syrup or sugar

1⁄16 teaspoon salt

3 egg yolks (optional)

1. First, be sure your ice cream maker bucket is completely frozen, which usually takes about 24 hours. If you like ice cream, I recommend storing the bucket in the freezer so that you can make ice cream at the drop of a hat.

2. Combine the cream, milk, maple syrup, salt, egg yolks, and the additional ingredients for your chosen flavor (see sidebar) in a blender or large mixing bowl. Whisk or blend until the mixture is very smooth and any hard ingredients, such as vanilla beans or chocolate chips, are broken up into extremely small pieces.

3. Place in the refrigerator and chill thoroughly, 1–2 hours.

4. Pour into your ice cream maker and freeze according to the manufacturer's directions, usually about 25–35 minutes.

5. Serve immediately for soft-serve style, or place the soft ice cream in the freezer and allow it to harden for 3–6 hours for a firmer result.

6. Store in the freezer for up to 1 week.

TRY DIFFERENT FLAVORS!

Vanilla: 2 tablespoons vanilla extract, or 1–2 vanilla beans, coarsely chopped

Chocolate Peanut Butter: ¼ cup cocoa powder (or more, to taste) and ½ cup peanut butter

Mint Chocolate Chip: 1 teaspoon spearmint or wintergreen extract (or more, to taste) and ¾ cup chocolate chips

Coconut: Replace the cream and milk with 3 cups full-fat coconut milk and add ¾ cup shredded coconut and 1 teaspoon vanilla extract

Strawberry: 6–8 strawberries, coarsely chopped and 1 tablespoon beet juice (optional)

Green Tea: Replace maple syrup with ¾ cup honey and add 3 tablespoons matcha green tea powder

Homemade Sprinkles

Making your own homemade sprinkles perhaps is overkill compared to all the other DIY projects you can do, but it's easy, it's fun, and it's satisfying. Besides, even small amounts of artificial coloring have been shown to increase hyperactivity, so making your own can help keep things at your next birthday party on a bit more of an even keel. You may certainly increase the ratio of powdered sugar to starch if you prefer sweeter sprinkles. Oh, and don't worry about the vodka in this recipe if making sprinkles for kids. The alcohol evaporates off completely, and using vodka instead of water speeds up the drying process.

HANDS-ON: 25 minutes

INACTIVE: 24 hours

READY IN: 24 hours

DIFFICULTY LEVEL: ★ ★ ★

YIELD: Serves 16; Makes 1 cup

COST PER SERVING: $

CALORIES: 33

FAT: 0 g

PROTEIN: 0 g

SODIUM: 0 mg

FIBER: 0 g

CARBOHYDRATES: 7 g

SUGAR: 3 g

½ **cup powdered sugar**

½ **cup cornstarch or arrowroot powder**

1 **teaspoon extract (almond, peppermint, vanilla, cherry, etc.; optional)**

Natural colorants (see sidebar)

1–2 **tablespoons vodka or water**

1. Place the powdered sugar and cornstarch into a sifter and sift 2–3 times into a medium-size bowl to make it fluffy and to remove every single clump.

2. If you're wanting multiple colors, divide the powder into equal portions in small bowls according to the number of colors you want. Add a few drops of extract to each, if desired; then add the colorant and vodka a few drops at a time until the mixture becomes a very thick, smooth paste. Have a large piece of wax paper or parchment paper, or a silicone baking mat, at the ready.

3. Spoon the paste into a piping bag with a very fine, single round tip or into a sandwich baggie. Cut a tiny corner off of the sandwich bag after the paste is inside, if using.

4. Pipe the paste into long, thin lines down the length of your prepared sheet. Set aside and let dry until the insides are completely dry—the line will snap when you break it, about 24 hours. If you are in a hurry, you can place them in a food dehydrator on the very lowest or "fan only" setting for 4–6 hours.

5. Break the lines into the desired size and store in an airtight container for 3–6 months.

NATURAL COLORANTS

Start with a small pinch or a few drops of these colorants and add more according to your desired shade.

YELLOW: turmeric

GREEN: matcha powder, spirulina powder, parsley juice, wheatgrass juice, spinach juice

RED: pure beet juice, pure pomegranate juice

PINK: 2–3 drops beet juice finished with vodka, pure cranberry juice

PURPLE: pure blueberry juice

BLUE: red cabbage leaves chopped and boiled for ½ hour—use the dyed water as your colorant

ORANGE: pure carrot juice

TAN: bentonite clay powder (this is an edible clay, but you may not want to use it in large quantities!)

BROWN: instant coffee granules, pure espresso, heavily steeped black tea

BLACK: activated charcoal powder (yes, it's safe to eat and even beneficial)

Chocolate Frosting

Okay, this recipe has a lot of sugar in it, but it's still a far cry from the one that comes in a plastic container from the store. It's just as thick and can be slathered on pretty much anything to make treats and desserts feel more festive. Be sure to use the darkest, bitterest chocolate you can find, as it balances the super saccharine flavor beautifully.

HANDS-ON: 20 minutes	
INACTIVE: none	
READY IN: 20 minutes	
DIFFICULTY LEVEL: ★ ★	
YIELD: Serves 28; Makes 7 cups	
COST PER SERVING: $ $	

GF V EF

CALORIES: 210

FAT: 14 g

PROTEIN: 1 g

SODIUM: 4 mg

FIBER: 1.5 g

CARBOHYDRATES: 21 g

SUGAR: 19 g

3 sticks (1½ cups) butter, at room temperature
8 ounces unsweetened chocolate, melted and cooled
4½ cups powdered sugar
¼ cup heavy cream
1 tablespoon vanilla extract

1. Using either the whisk or the paddle attachment, cream the butter in an electric mixer on high for 6–7 minutes until it's very pale in color, scraping down the sides of the bowl as needed. Reduce speed to low and slowly pour in the chocolate.

2. Add a few spoonfuls of the powdered sugar. When it's completely incorporated, add the cream and the extract.

3. Continue to add the powdered sugar a few spoonfuls at a time. When all the sugar has been incorporated, increase the speed to medium and cream for another 4–5 minutes until the frosting is very light and fluffy.

4. Store in an airtight container in the refrigerator for up to 1 week.

White Frosting

This frosting is just as sweet as the chocolate frosting listed here, but it doesn't have the balance of the bitter chocolate to offset it. Thus, be sure to flavor it heavily so that your flavor can actually shine through all that sugary fluff. And while this may not be fancy, it's a fabulous stand-in for the store-bought variety, and you can take heart that it's preservative-free and uses nourishing natural fats rather than industrialized, hydrogenated oils. That's not free license to eat the whole batch (no matter how tempted you may be), but it will certainly satisfy your sweet tooth for a decade or two.

HANDS-ON: 20 minutes

INACTIVE: none

READY IN: 20 minutes

DIFFICULTY LEVEL: ★ ★

YIELD: Serves 26; Makes 6½ cups

COST PER SERVING: $ $

GF V EF

CALORIES: 182

FAT: 11 g

PROTEIN: 0 g

SODIUM: 3 mg

FIBER: 0 g

CARBOHYDRATES: 20 g

SUGAR: 20 g

3 sticks (1½ cups) butter, at room temperature, or ½ cup butter plus 1 cup palm shortening

4½ cups powdered sugar

¼ cup heavy cream

2 tablespoons flavored extract (vanilla, lemon, almond, etc.)

1. Using either the whisk or the paddle attachment, cream the butter in an electric mixer on high for 6–7 minutes until it's very pale in color, scraping down the sides of the bowl as needed.

2. Reduce speed to low. Add a few spoonfuls of the powdered sugar. When it's completely incorporated, add the cream and the extract.

3. Continue to add the powdered sugar a few spoonfuls at a time. When all the sugar has been incorporated, increase the speed to medium and cream for another 4–5 minutes until the frosting is very light and fluffy.

4. Store in an airtight container in the refrigerator for up to 1 week.

Simple Sugar Syrup

High fructose corn syrup is one of the most pervasive—and certainly one of the most vilified—ingredients in processed food today. Due to its ease of use, it shows up in everything from cola to baked beans to crackers. The problem is, however, that high fructose corn syrup is linked to a large number of health problems, ranging from belly fat to diabetes. This recipe for a neutral-flavored, liquid sugar is a great substitute for corn syrup. A liquid sugar keeps certain sweet desserts, such as fudge and marshmallows, from becoming grainy while they set, resulting in smooth, delectable treats. This recipe does require a candy thermometer, which can be found for only $3–$4 at most mass merchandisers.

HANDS-ON: 30 minutes

INACTIVE: 1 hour

READY IN: 1½ hours

DIFFICULTY LEVEL:
★ ★ ★ ★

YIELD: Serves 16; Makes 2 cups

COST PER SERVING: $

CALORIES: 122

FAT: 0 g

PROTEIN: 0 g

SODIUM: 10 mg

FIBER: 0 g

CARBOHYDRATES: 31 g

SUGAR: 31 g

1 cup water

2½ cups cane sugar

1½ teaspoons lemon juice, or ¼ teaspoon citric acid

¹⁄₁₆ teaspoon salt

1. Place all of the ingredients in a large saucepan and stir to completely moisten the sugar. Place the pan over medium-high heat.

2. As the sugar comes to a boil, continually brush down the sides of the pan with a wet pastry brush as drops of sugar splatter—but do not stir the sugar at any point.

3. Boil the syrup until it reaches 238°F—the syrup should still be clear and not have begun to caramelize or turn amber. Remove the pan from the heat and let it sit undisturbed until it has cooled completely, about 1 hour.

4. Gently pour the cooled syrup into a glass jar and store for up to 3 months. Be forewarned that the syrup can very easily crystallize, which can happen due to slight agitation, a drop of water dripping onto the syrup, or if you happen to store it in a very cool place. Just remelt it in a very hot water bath and use it as desired.

Peppermint Patties

Even though honey and chocolate should be enjoyed in small quantities, coconut oil is a deeply nourishing plant-based fat that is healthy in every sense of the word. So if you have a sweet tooth and regularly like to snack on sweet treats, consider keeping a batch of these in the freezer at all times, so at least you'll have a healthy option when cravings hit. Also, if you live in a warm climate, be forewarned that these are not as shelf-stable as the store-bought version that has additives to account for temperature changes: It's best to keep these in the freezer until serving.

HANDS-ON: 25 minutes

INACTIVE: 1 hour

READY IN: 1½ hours

DIFFICULTY LEVEL: ★ ★ ★

YIELD: Serves 12; Makes 12 patties

COST PER SERVING: $ $

GF V DF EF

CALORIES: 135

FAT: 11 g

PROTEIN: 0 g

SODIUM: 1 g

FIBER: 0.5 g

CARBOHYDRATES: 10 g

SUGAR: 9.5 g

½ cup coconut oil, soft but still solid

¼ cup honey

¾ teaspoon peppermint extract

½–1 cup dark chocolate chips, melted

1 tablespoon cocoa butter (optional)

1 tablespoon coconut milk (optional)

1. Blend the coconut oil, honey, and peppermint extract in a food processor or whisk vigorously by hand until smooth.

2. Spoon by heaping tablespoons into mini-muffin tins and smooth down the top as you are able. Place in the freezer for at least 30 minutes to harden.

3. Melt the chocolate and cocoa butter over very low heat, adding coconut milk if needed to thin it to a consistency that's easy for dipping. When the chocolate is melted, set aside until cool to touch but still liquid. Have a plate or parchment paper at the ready.

4. Pop the coconut oil patties out of the muffin tin; then submerge them in the chocolate with a fork and place them on the plate. Return them to the freezer to firm up the chocolate, about 10 minutes.

5. Store in an airtight container in the freezer for up to 1 month.

Almond Roca

This classic buttercrunch toffee will keep you coming back for more because of its richness and delightful texture. The lemon juice in this recipe is used to keep the toffee as smooth as possible, like corn syrup would. If you live in a damp climate, a sugar syrup is much more trustworthy than a honey-based one to maintain its shape over the course of several days. Likewise, if you live in a damp climate, you can substitute up to 2 tablespoons of the butter with palm shortening to keep the candy from weeping, but the flavor won't be as rich.

HANDS-ON: 30 minutes

INACTIVE: 1 hour

READY IN: 1½ hours

DIFFICULTY LEVEL:
★ ★ ★ ★

YIELD: Serves 24; Makes 24 bars

COST PER SERVING: $ $

GF V EF

CALORIES: 139

FAT: 9 g

PROTEIN: 2 g

SODIUM: 52 mg

FIBER: 1 g

CARBOHYDRATES: 14 g

SUGAR: 12 g

1½ cups toasted whole almonds, coarsely chopped
8 tablespoons (1 stick) butter
¾ cup packed brown sugar or unrefined cane sugar
½ teaspoon lemon juice
½ teaspoon salt
1 teaspoon vanilla
2 ounces cocoa butter (optional)
8 ounces dark or milk chocolate

1. Place a sheet of parchment paper in a 9" × 5" loaf pan and smooth it into the corners. Make it as flat as possible. Set aside.

2. Grind the almonds into a coarse meal and place in a medium bowl. Set aside.

3. In a heavy-bottomed saucepan, melt the butter over medium-high heat; then add the sugar, lemon juice, and salt, and stir until the sugar dissolves.

4. Once the sugar melts, start a timer and boil the syrup for 7 minutes, stirring constantly with a wooden spoon. If you're using a thermometer, take the syrup off the heat once it reaches 305°F. If you don't have a thermometer (or just to double-check), have a bowl of cold water nearby. When the timer dings at 7 minutes, drip a drop of syrup into the bowl; then squish it with your fingers. If it's soft, it's not ready, but if it beads up into a hard candy ball, it's ready.

5. When the syrup is ready, stir in the vanilla; then scrape the butter-sugar syrup into the prepared loaf pan—it should be in a layer about ½" thick.

6. When the syrup is cool enough to hold an indentation, about 5 minutes, use a sharp knife to cut the toffee into 24 bars by cutting one long cut down the length of the toffee and twelve cuts across the short width. Repeat this step about 5–7 minutes later as the toffee hardens.

7. Once the toffee is cool enough to handle, lift out the parchment paper and cut it into pieces along the lines you made. Smooth out or break off any sharp edges.

8. When the toffee is completely cooled, melt the cocoa butter over medium-low heat. Add the chocolate and turn off the heat. Stir occasionally until the chocolate is completely melted; then let sit until it's cool but still liquid.

9. Set a cooling rack over a piece of parchment paper and have the chopped almonds at hand.

10. Dip each piece of hard toffee in the melted chocolate; then roll it in the bowl of nuts. Place on the cooling rack. Repeat until all the toffee pieces are coated with chocolate and nuts and let them sit until the chocolate is completely hardened. (If you're working in a warm room, pop them in the refrigerator to set the chocolate, about 10 minutes.)

11. For best results, store in an airtight container in the refrigerator for up to 1 month. Serve at room temperature.

APPENDIX

Finding Ingredients and Supplies

Wanting to know where you can find ingredients, supplies, and more information about feeding your family simply and well? Saw an ingredient in one of the recipes that you're not sure where to find? Here are a few resources and ideas to get you started.

Herbs and Spices

Mountain Rose Herbs: *www.mountainroseherbs.com*

Frontier Co-op: *www.frontiercoop.com*

Morton & Bassett: *www.mortonbassett.com*

Bulk Herb Store: *www.bulkherbstore.com*

Organic and Natural Foods

Frontier Co-op: *www.frontiercoop.com*

Wilderness Family Naturals: *www.wilderness familynaturals.com*

Azure Standard: *www.azurestandard.com*

Redmond Trading: *www.redmondtrading.com*

Amazon.com: *www.amazon.com/grocery*

Cultures and Cheesemaking Supplies

Cultures for Health: *www.culturesforhealth.com*

New England Cheesemaking Supply: *www.cheesemaking .com*

Leeners: *www.leeners.com*

Grass-Fed Beef Gelatin (Kosher)

Great Lakes Gelatin: *www.greatlakesgelatin.com*

Bernard Jensen International: *www.bernardjensen.com*

Amazon.com: *www.amazon.com*

Buckwheat Flour

Anson Mills: *www.ansonmills.com*

Cold Mountain Japanese-style buckwheat flour: available in-store only

King Arthur Flour: *www.kingarthurflour.com*

Amazon.com: *www.amazon.com*

Mother of Vinegar

Leeners: *www.leeners.com*

Palm Shortening & Coconut Oil

Spectrum Naturals: *www.spectrumorganics.com*

Tropical Traditions: *www.tropicaltraditions.com*

Amazon.com: *www.amazon.com*

Sustainable Meat, Fish, and Seafood

i love blue sea: *www.ilovebluesea.com*

U.S. Wellness Meats: *www.uswellnessmeats.com*

Eat Wild: *www.eatwild.com*

Fresh Eggs, Milk, and Produce

Local Harvest: *www.localharvest.com*

Farms and Markets: *www.farmsandmarkets.com*

Eat Wild: *www.eatwild.com*

Sustainable Table: *www.sustainabletable.org*

Craigslist Want Ads: *www.craigslist.com*

Real Milk: *www.realmilk.com*

Index

Acknowledgments

Even though I came up with the ingredients for these recipes by flipping over every box, can, and package I could get my hands on, the techniques I employed have come by learning from so many others who have gone before me. Through the years, I have checked out countless cookbooks from the library and filled my shelves with textbooks from professional cooking schools, and it would be remiss of me not to mention those authors who have taught me so much.

My thanks go to Nancy Silverton, the 52+ chefs and authors of *The Professional Chef*, James Peterson, Tish Boyle, Julia Child, Jim Lahey, Christopher Idone, Renèe Roux Underkoffler, Brother Victor-Antoine d'Avila-Latourrette, the authors and contributors of the Mennonite Central Committee's *More-with-Less*, Dr. Weston A. Price, Sally Fallon, and Mary Enig, PhD.

And of course, my even deeper thanks for the vision of this book go to friends and family:

To my mother, who can get a nutritious meal on the table faster than I can write this sentence and who taught me that feeding a family frugally is both an art and a noble calling.

To my husband, who shares my vision for sustainable agriculture and healthy food systems and who understands that my "love language" is food. Richard, I love you and eagerly look forward to continuing this grand adventure together.

To Valerie Mangrum, for teaching me to think of cooking as an art form, to strive to cook well, and to use good food as a way of welcoming guests eagerly.

To Debbie Anderson, at whose table there's always room for one more.

To Tanja Traber, for teaching me that cake doesn't have to be fancy to make every day special.

And to the chefs (yes, Denis, that includes you) who have let me look over their shoulders while they make a classic sauce or fillet a large fish in two minutes flat, I am indebted to you for the skills and confidence you have given me in my own kitchen.

And of course, I want to thank those who helped me significantly while I wrote this book. This was certainly not a lone endeavor:

My parents, John and Mary Frankhauser, who cared for my children so joyfully and lovingly for weeks on end while I buried myself in writing and research and who have been an endless source of encouragement.

My parents-in-law, Simon and Michelle Faber, who have provided a home for our family for the last few years, which has allowed us to plan and dream toward running our own farm and in that way stewarding the many gifts God has given us, and of which writing this book certainly is a part.

My mother-in-law, who shares a love of good food and laughing together over a glass of wine.

Lisa and Rachel, both of whom cheerfully welcomed my children on very short notice on numerous occasions so that I could write and who tested recipe after recipe—your joyful hospitality is such a gift!

Tova and Maggie, who provided much inspiration, childcare, and hours of conversation that helped me think more clearly, pray more fervently, and write more creatively. I am deeply grateful to both of you for your presence in my life.

Stephanie, who gave me a deadline for my first cookbook and inspired me to do it well.

Karen, who helped me see the simple acts of choosing to cloth diaper and make my own yogurt as gateways to a more intentional, thoughtful, natural way of living.

The 454 recipe testers who tested these recipes and gave me invaluable feedback.

And lastly, the fabulous editorial staff at Adams Media, in particular Maria Ribas, Diane Garcia, Ross Neuenfeldt, and Erin Dawson for being able to take my chicken scratches, rough drafts, and grand ideas and transform them into the lovely, organized book you now have in your hands.